OMNIVM · LVX · CIVIVM

BOSTON
PUBLIC
LIBRARY

The Dream of Reality

Heinz von Foerster's Constructivism

The Dream of Reality

Heinz von Foerster's Constructivism

Lynn Segal

Mental Research Institute,
Palo Alto, California

W · W · NORTON & COMPANY
New York *London*

Published simultaneously in Canada by Penguin Books Canada Ltd, 2801 John Street, Markham, Ontario L3R 1B4

Printed in the United States of America.

First Edition

Library of Congress Cataloging-in-Publication Data

Segal, Lynn.
  The dream of reality.

  Bibliography: p.
  Includes index.
  1. Von Foerster, Heinz, 1911-   — Contributions in
theory of knowledge.   2. Knowledge, Theory of — History —
20th century.   I. Title.
BD161.S39   1986   121'.092'4   85-31025

ISBN   0-393-70026-7

W. W. Norton & Company, Inc., 500 Fifth Avenue, New York, N.Y. 10110
W. W. Norton & Company Ltd., 37 Great Russell Street, London WC1B 3NU

1   2   3   4   5   6   7   8   9   0

ABOUT THE AUTHOR

Lynn Segal, a licensed clinical social worker, is a research associate of the Mental Research Institute (MRI) and a member of that institute's Brief Therapy Project. He received his B.A. degree in psychology from Hofstra University (1966) and his M.S.W. degree in social work form Adelphi University (1968). He was the recipient of the Don D. Jackson Memorial Award in 1977, was one of the organizers and co-leaders of the El Camino Hospital Pain Program, and is past chairman of the MRI Training Committee. Presently, he divides his professional time between training others in brief therapy and family systems work, doing research in psychotherapy, and maintaining a private practice in Palo Alto. He has conducted training workshops throughout the United States and in Europe.

He is also the co-author (with Fisch and Weakland) of *The Tactics of Change: Doing Therapy Briefly.*

REALITY – THE EIGHTEENTH CAMEL

A travelling mullah was riding on his camel to Medina, when he saw several camels standing next to a group of three young men who clearly were in distress.

"What befell you, my friends?" he asked, and the eldest replied, "Our father died."

"Be he blessed by Allah. I sympathize with you. But he must have left you something in his will."

"Yes," said the young man, "these seventeen camels. That's all he had."

"Rejoice! What then ails you?"

"You see," the eldest brother continued, "his will says I should get one-half of his possessions, my younger brother one-third, and the youngest here one-ninth. But however we try to distribute these camels, it never works out."

"Is this all that troubles you, my friends?" the mullah said. "Then take my camel for a moment and let's see what we can do."

With 18 camels now the eldest brother got one-half, that is, nine camels, and nine were left. The next in line got one-third of the 18 camels, that is, six, and three were left. Since the youngest brother got one-ninth of the 18 camels, that is, two, one camel was left. It was that of the mullah, who mounted it and rode away, waving the happy brothers good-bye.

To this Heinz Von Foerster says: "Reality, like the eighteenth camel, is needed to become superfluous."

Contents

Foreword

The Heinz von Foerster who travels among family therapists, who speaks here and is invited there, is an invention of Paul Watzlawick.

I met my inventor for the first time more than ten years ago in California. My services to the University of Illinois, after about 30 years, had come to an end, and I was looking for a place where my wife and I could retire and spend the rest of our lives *procul negotiis*. Paul Watzlawick first introduced himself over the telephone with an Austrian dialect similar to mine, telling me about common friends, for instance, Gregory Bateson, and common interests, for instance, pathologies in logic. Soon afterwards we met, and in our mutual enjoyment of obviating the obvious and doubting certainty the seeds for a friendship were planted.

When he invited me to speak on the occasion of the Second Don D. Jackson Memorial Conference to members and guests of the Mental Research Institute of Palo Alto, I accepted. On the first evening Gregory Bateson gave his address to the plenary session, and I on the second.

In Bateson's lectures there were always some points that impressed me very much. Somebody asked him whether or not a certain something was the cause for another certain something. Roughly he replied that "cause," "fear," "tension," etc., are the inappropriate words. It is the *un-real* problem to ask whether the cause of this phenomenology is to be found in physics, physiology, psychology, genetics, etc. And then he said (and now I quote): "These divisions are fashionable. But they are insane."

What impressed me as crucial was that he did not say that these divisions are useless, or misleading, or blind alleys, or whatever. He said they are "insane." He added that what he is aiming at and looking for is an epistemology in which these concepts are woven into the whole epistemology.

Later I overhead some participants commenting on Bateson's style of giving puzzling and mystifying answers to simple and clear questions. Hence, I opened my presentation, entitled, "Contradictions, Paradoxes, Vicious Circles, and other Creative Devices," by saying that the trouble with the utterances of great men is that they are so transparent. But, paradoxically, what is transparent cannot be seen. Therefore, my plan is to make some of these issues opaque so that they can be seen, at least for a moment, before they slip away when clarified.

Apparently this strategy had appeal. On the other hand, I became acquainted and fascinated with the spectrum of problems that were discussed at this conference; they touched on problems in philosophy and theories of knowing and communicating in which we, at the Biological Computer Laboratory of the University of Illinois, were very much interested. In essence, these are problems of cognition, and it was, and still is, this point of common competence and ignorance that kept the dialogue between the therapeutic profession and me alive and well.

Also, it came to pass that a friend and co-worker-and-thinker of mine, Humberto Maturana, the "neurophilosopher" as he liked to be called, participated in, and enforced the biological end of this dialogue, in which all parties recognized the need for a language that includes the observer (therapist) in the ongoing process of interaction and intervention, a posture that an orthodox frame of thought, based on the independence and exclusion of the observer—the idea of "objectivity"—does not provide.

On the many occasions that later offered themselves for continuing this dialogue I had finally the opportunity to see through the oneway mirror for family therapy in action. Most of the time I was sitting on the edge of my chair in the darkened observation room, watching the unfolding of a universe, the family, experiencing the various blindnesses of its members toward each other, even blindness regarding their own blindness: they don't see that they don't see.

On one occasion, when my colleagues had left the observation room and I was left alone, I had a most surprising and revealing experience. I became curious about whether I could detect unspoken clues of communication better without the audio on. So I turned it off. What then happened was very eerie indeed. Here were five people, sitting quietly around a table, moving, as in slow motion, to turn one face to another, lips, from time to time, parting and closing; the kid, completely detached, biting his nails, looking over the place, stops only once, moves his lips, and then continues biting his nails. . . . This goes on for an eternity of 30 minutes. Suddenly the therapist rises, the others follow; there are smiles, hand shakes, and a social charade, where all is understood, concludes the session.

I learned later that this case came to a successful conclusion. Apparently, it must have been the noises I could not hear, that were modulated by the parting and closing of lips, that provided a realm for all to re-invent their relations to others, the world, and the image of themselves.

Of course, I could have used the word "language" to account for these fundamental changes, but then the magic of language would not have become apparent.

Whenever I speak in public I first say what I am going to tell, then tell it, and finally say what it was. Usually I stick to my prediction: I tell what I had promised to tell. But in my recapitulations I aim at expanding the general context by turning the subject matter around, tossing new light on some points, inventing different examples, etc.

When Lynn Segal decided to use video and audiotapes of some of my lectures, together with my notes augmented by his own, for presenting the core of these ideas in a well ordered story with a beginning, a middle, and an end, I was skeptical. On several occasions I had presented my points in a series of four or five installments, where in each I recapitulated all the earlier ones; I felt that Lynn Segal's task was more like unraveling the secrets of the Rubik cube than narrating a story about the evolution of some ideas. On second thought, however, this task could also be seen as an exercise in inventing a reality.

In this case, my hope is to have the role of the eighteenth camel. But without the wisdom of the mullah the camel has no role. Fortunately, the mullah has been found: it is Lynn Segal! Here are my compliments to him and my thanks.

Heinz von Foerster
February 1986

Foreword

Lynn Segal has taken upon himself the exceedingly difficult task of presenting the life work of a famous scientist, translated into a readable nontechnical language, in a relatively slim volume. The difficulty is compounded by the fact that Heinz von Foerster defies any simple categorization, as he transcends the traditional academic boundaries of scientific disciplines. Like a belated renaissance man or — if one prefers — the forerunner of an era in which natural and humanistic sciences will begin to converge, he fascinates his listeners and his readers by his encyclopedic knowledge, coupled with the ease with which he establishes totally new connections, and thereby forces us to question our traditional ways of conceptualizing the world. This is the process that Arthur Koestler called *biosociation* and credited with man's creative power.

Heinz von Foerster is one of the leading members of that incredibly gifted group of scientists who in 1949 got together under the auspices of the Josiah Macy Jr. Foundation for the purpose of studying "circular causal feedback mechanisms in biological and social systems." It was Warren McCulloch, the chairman of these meetings, who invited Heinz von Foerster to present a theory of memory which he had developed when still in Vienna, and which was, without his knowing it at the time, built on what are now called *cybernetic* principles.

What thus began as the study of dynamic processes of a general nature soon revealed its specific importance for the understanding of man and his social interactions. The realization that the observer, the observed phenomenon *and* the process of observation itself form a totality, which can be decomposed into its elements only on pain of absurd reifications, has far-reaching implications for our understanding of man and his problems — especially of the ways in which he literally "constructs" his reality, then reacts to it as if it existed independently of him "out there," and eventually may arrive at the startling awareness that his reactions are *both* the effect and the cause of his reality construction. This "curved space" of human experience of the world and of himself, this *closure* — as Heinz von Foerster calls it — finds its symbolic expression in the Ouroboros, the snake that bites its own tail, or its poetic expression in the words of T. S. Eliot, for whom "the end of all our exploring will be to arrive where we started and know the place for the first time."

Lynn Segal has succeeded in making this also the structure of this book — whose last chapter "curves back" on the first and introduces the reader into what he has just read — as if it were for the first time.

Paul Watzlawick

Preface

There is a current view that philosophy should be left
to philosophers, sociology to the sociologists, and death
to the dead. I believe this is one of the great heresies —
and tyrannies — of our time.

— John Fowles[1]

Heinz von Foerster is a cybernetician, a mathematician, a
physicist, and a philosopher. I first heard him speak in San Francisco on June 30, 1978 at the Mental Research Institute's bien-
nial family therapy conference. His talk afforded both staff and
participants the rare opportunity of hearing a cybernetician discuss fundamental concepts family therapists had borrowed from
cybernetics to model family behavior.

Von Foerster is an electrifying speaker with a depth of knowledge that he presents with enthusiasm and humor. He talks very
fast, with a strong Viennese accent, packing every sentence with
a wealth of ideas. In the 1950s, someone affectionately wrote a
science fiction story about him in which a special computer transcribed his intense speech into normal understandable language.
No wonder my colleagues were baffled by his presentation. "Perhaps brilliant," they said, "but extremely difficult to comprehend." Although I had a similar experience, I was fascinated with
his material. I just had to understand what he was talking about.

Fortunately, in the years that followed, our paths continued to cross, providing additional opportunities for me to hear him speak. As I became more familiar with his ideas, I found them useful in my work as a psychotherapist and teacher. Von Foerster transforms philosophical and psychological ideas from seemingly impractical and boring material into useful conceptual tools. His work helped me to gain a deeper understanding of how language and logic shape thinking, particularly in the models used by psychotherapists to carry out their professional tasks. It also became increasingly clear, that von Foerster, like Freud, had something to offer anyone who would take the time and effort to understand his ideas. Thus, I became convinced that these ideas should be brought to the attention of a wider audience.

THE BOOK

Two events led to my writing this book. First, the Mental Research Institute (MRI) acquired a collection of von Foerster's lectures, recorded on both audio and videotape. MRI's tape library provided a representative sample of von Foerster's material, containing most of the arguments, ideas, stories, and illustrations I had heard in his talks. Second, I purchased a computer system with excellent word processing capabilities. My secretary, who had the identical word processor, could transcribe audiotape segments of his lectures onto computer disk, which I could edit on my own system.

I told von Foerster I wanted to edit his lectures into a book. He was enthusiastic and supportive, suggesting that I let him examine a sample of my work. He liked my initial drafts, and in the summer of 1982 I set out to finish the project.

The following year, after editing the majority of the material, we realized the book had serious problems. I had transformed the transcription into Lynn Segal's interpretation of Heinz von Foerster. Second, I had followed the outline he used for his lectures. Although well-suited for a verbal presentation, it was, unfortunately, inappropriate for a book, necessitating a major reorganization of the material.

Von Foerster liked how I presented his ideas and my proposed outline for reorganizing the material. He felt, however, that the book should be my own project. He wanted me to address the reader. As he put it, "I want to set you free to write your own book." He offered to give me all his materials — diagrams, examples, references, stories, etc. He would be available to discuss ideas whenever the need arose, but I must tell my own story. The writing and interpretation must be mine. In other words, my role would change from editor to author — the sole author.

Initially, his suggestion left me extremely anxious. I had no formal training in philosophy, mathematics or neurophysiology. In fact, part of my motivation for editing his lectures was to deepen my grasp of these subjects. After some anxious deliberation, I decided to accept his generous offer if we could reach a compromise. I would continue my original plan — presenting the von Foerster's lecture material in written form — but, rather than editing his lectures, the book would be my report about them.

A NOTE TO THE READER

The shift from edited transcript to my report about von Foerster's constructivism requires that the reader take note of the following: First, many sentences written in the third person evolved from the original transcript, i.e., von Foerster's own words. Second, quotations without reference number are *my interpretation* of what von Foerster said. Their liberal use is my attempt to convey the man as well as his ideas. Third, quotations with reference numbers have been edited for clarity. Fourth, all diagrams and most examples are von Foerster's. Fifth, although the book represents material from several von Foerster lectures, it does not claim to be a complete or comprehensive presentation of von Foerster's thinking or of constructivism and related subjects. Sixth, although von Foerster has read and approved the final manuscript, I take full responsibility for presenting the material.

Additionally, as this work progressed, I decided to include many of the ideas of Humberto Maturana, a Chilian neurophysiologist, von Foerster's close friend and colleague. Maturana's work complements and expands von Foerster's thesis.

Finally, in my never ending search to make this material comprehensible, I chose to avoid the awkwardness inherent in such usage as he/she or his or her. No slight is intended in my use of the masculine tense. However, the reader may encounter an occasional sentence that appears sexist, and for this I apologize.

ACKNOWLEDGMENTS

Rarely is a book the work of one person. We are the recipients of a long history of ideas. Additionally, our family, friends, colleagues, students, and secretaries usually play a significant part in the process. Finally, there is the interplay of author and editor(s), shaping the manuscript into the final product. Although I am the sole author of this book, it could not have been completed without the help of many people and I would like to take this opportunity to thank them.

To Heinz and Mai von Foerster, I would like to express my deep appreciation and gratitude for all the affection, encouragement, and support they have shown me throughout this project. They have given freely of their time, energy, ideas, and editorial skills. I could not have written this book without their assistance. My true reward for this project was spending time in their company.

To Paul Watzlawick, thank you for taking time to write a foreword for this book.

To Carol Wilder, my friend and colleague, thank you for allowing me to publish the excellent interview you conducted with Dr. von Foerster.

To Sharon Lucas, thank you for transcribing audiotapes which were difficult to hear and understand.

To John Herr and David Kahn, a special thanks for all those delightful hours discussing this material, helping me clarify my own thinking.

To my colleagues, friends, and students who have read portions of this manuscript, Ann Brandewie, Neil Brast, Freda Carpenter, Joyce Emamjomeh, Richard Grossman, Maria Kent, Allen Vanderwell, Marty Weiner, and Lenora Yuen, thank you for the constructive comments and suggestions.

Lynn Segal
Mental Research Institute
Palo Alto, California

The Dream of Reality

Heinz von Foerster's Constructivism

Introduction

"God save us from what man does in the name of good."
— Paladin, *Have Gun will Travel*[1]

The constructivism of Heinz von Foerster is concerned with the convergence of two central themes: 1) how we know what we know, and 2) an abiding concern for the present state of the world and its humanity. For the constructivist, the dreams of reason denote a common denominator running through our language and logic, manifest as a wish for what we call "reality" to have a certain shape and form. The wish has several dimensions.

First, we wish reality to *exist independently* of us, we who observe it. Second, we wish reality be *discoverable*, to reveal itself to us. We wish to know its secrets, i.e., how it works. Third, we wish these secrets to be *lawful*, so we can predict and ultimately control reality. Fourth, we wish for *certainty*; we wish to know that what we have discovered about reality is true.

Radical constructivism challenges this wish, thus taking on the unpopular job of shattering the fantasy of an objective reality. Constructivists argue that there are no observations — i.e., no data, no laws of nature, no external objects — *independent* of observers. The lawfulness and certainty of all natural phenomena are properties of the describer, not of what is being described. The logic of the world is the logic of the description of the world.

Constructivism identifies, for all who care to look through the lens of its epistemology, the limits of what we can know. However, the primary aim of the constructivist is not to find fault with traditional epistemologies, but to account for cognition, the totality of our mental faculties, without first assuming an independent reality.

Constructivists argue that to understand the world we must begin by understanding ourselves, i.e., the observers. Herein lies the dilemma. We cannot account for the observer in the manner followed by most biologists, psychologists, neurophysiologists, etc. Their traditional methods of science separate the observer from his observations, forbidding self-reference to preserve objectivity. If we are to understand perception, the observer must be able to account for himself, for his own ability to perceive. Thus, unlike traditional scientists and philosophers, constructivists embrace self-reference and recursion. And, since everything that is said in a scientific account is said with language, constructivism aims to formulate an epistemology that can account for how language comes into being.

Embracing the constructivist position is potentially liberating, allowing one to tap his or her creative potential. This position rejects the belief in one right answer to the exclusion of all other possibilities. A richness of choice is the hallmark of an adaptable or, in the case of human beings, healthy system. Consider von Foerster's ethical imperative: "Act always so as to increase the number of choices." Or his moral imperative: "A is better off when B is better off." For the constructivist, life is a non-zero sum game: all players win or all players lose. Cooperation, not competition, is the sine qua non of social existence. The price of this world view, however, is that one must replace the notion of objectivity with that of responsibility.

In the final analysis, constructivism's moral concern is to reduce monsters of reason — fascism, genocide, nuclear war, and totalitarianism — by revealing the nature of the dreamer.

HOW THIS BOOK IS ORGANIZED

Chapter 1, "The Myth of Objectivity," introduces the problem of objectivity: What can we know beyond our experience? The historical, philosophical, and scientific implications of this problem are examined in light of how our scientific worship of "objectivity" influences our understanding of ourselves and the world.

Chapter 2, "The Difficulties of Language," discusses how language structures our logical devices — syllogisms, causality, etc. — and invents "things," leading us to believe that we discover "things" in the real world rather than invent them.

Chapter 3, "Maturana and the Observer," introduces Humberto Maturana's system for handling the problem of objectivity when doing science (accounting for observed phenomena), particularly when studying cognition and the operation of the central nervous system.

Taken together, Chapters 4, 5, 6, and 7 attempt to explain how we are able to have such a rich experience of the world when our senses do not encode the nature of the stimuli that excite them. These four chapters integrate several concepts — computation, biocomputation, the nervous system, and closure — in attempting to account for cognition *without* assuming that the objects of perception exist independently of the observer. Thus, the entire cognitive equation is turned on its head. The scientific question asked is as follows: What kind of a world is produced by a closed or inputless nervous system? In other words, given a closed nervous system, what is the nature of cognition?

Chapter 4 discusses the nervous system, its structure and function. Chapter 5 introduces the concept of computation, its embodiment in computing machines, and the use of "logical" machines to model cognitive processes. Chapter 6, "Biocomputation," applies computational concepts to the central nervous system. Chapter 7 introduces and applies the concepts of closure and infinite recursion to the operations of the nervous system. Thus, the nervous system is discussed as a closed sensorimotor neuronal network which computes a stable reality. The appendix contains an interview Carol Wilder conducted with von Foerster at his home in Pescadero, California. Von Foerster describes his childhood, his emigration to America and many of the luminaries he has had the pleasure of knowing and working with during the past 45 years.

Finally, the reader should take note: von Foerster's work, a framework for understanding cognition, is "not so much a completed edifice, but rather a clearly shaped space, where the major building lines are established and the access clearly indicated."[2] Von Foerster's work opens more doors than it closes.[3]

1

The Myth of Objectivity

> What we know is generally considered to be the result of our exploration of the real world, of the way things really are. . . . How we know is a far more vexing problem. To solve it, the mind needs to step outside itself, so to speak; for at this point we are no longer with facts that apparently exist independently of us in the outside world . . .
>
> — Paul Watzlawick[1]

> Cloquet hated reality but realized it was still the only place to get a good steak.
>
> — Woody Allen[2]

> The fish is the last one to know that it lives in the water.
>
> — Chinese aphorism[3]

The problem of objectivity centers on the question: What can we know about reality? The dominant epistemology (theory of knowledge) underlying most accounts of cognition begins with the assumption that the world, i.e., objective reality, exists independently of we who observe it. Thus, the logical imperative for the philosopher, psychologist, or neurophysiologist is to account for how we perceive and know about such a world.

Although we can linguistically assert the notion of objectivity — knowledge of an object, independent of observation — there is no way of proving reality's existence or confirming our "knowledge." Philosophers of science are well aware of this dilemma and, when pressed, will admit that scientists must simply grant the objectivity of reality if they are to do science and offer scientific explanations of observed phenomena.

This book shall make a radical departure from these assumptions. It will construct an epistemology that argues that what we can know is a function of the observer rather than what is observed. However, before constructing this epistemology, we need to closely examine the problem of objectivity from semantic, philosophical, and neurological perspectives. Thus, the question now before us is: What is the notion "objectivity" and why do constructivists reject it?

POINTS OF DEPARTURE

Our first point of departure is examining how language generates the notion of objectivity. Each of us is an observer, a biological system capable of observation. Observers live in language the way fish live in water. Language is the medium of our cognitive existence. "Everything that can be said is said by an observer to another observer, who may be him or herself."[4]

Language uses symbols to represent *things*, which may be either concrete or conceptual. For instance, there is nothing chair-like about a chair or table-like about a table. Using symbols requires agreement among observers. Speaking a language means sharing agreements about the perception of "reality," a word whose Latin root comes from the noun *res*, meaning *thing*.[5] If we take a closer look at the term *res*, however, we find that *res* refers to matters of business and property. The Latin root *res* appears in the word "republic," the public ownership; *res* defines what is owned. The realtor sells realties, those things which are immobile. Hence, *res* is essentially a legal concept.

We assume that "reality" contains things or objects which exist independently of the observer. At least this is the common belief. Most linguists argue that language arises from our learning to name these objects. To know them with the senses is to *perceive* them, a word derived from the Latin word meaning "to grasp." To perceptually grasp an *object* is to perceive it. Conversely, the words "illusion" and "hallucination" denote perceiving things not there, i.e., misperceiving reality.[6] Psychiatrists describe patients who hallucinate as being "out of touch with reality." So the terms "reality," "perception," "illusion," and "hallucination" are circularly interdependent, giving each other their meaning.

Language implicitly differentiates the true from the false by distinguishing between perception and illusion. The word "objective" denotes knowledge of the thing itself, the way it really is, independent of observation. By definition, objective knowledge is *discovered* rather than invented. When something residing in reality is discovered, the discovery is said to be "true." Objectivity is the *summum bonum* of the scientific method, and scientists, having taken over a function formerly performed by priests and shamans, have become our official liaisons with reality.

OBJECTIVE KNOWLEDGE

But can observers have objective knowledge? The clue to solving this problem centers on the question: How good is one's knowledge, one's perceptions of reality? As von Glasersfeld[7] explains, as early as the 6th century B.C., philosophers defined knowledge as that which depicts or explains something else. Knowledge was deemed correct when judged equivalent, isomorphic, or characteristic of the original phenomenon. He describes this relationship as ironic, i.e., knowledge is a picture that represents something else.

Naturally, explains von Glasersfeld, philosophers soon wondered: How good is my knowledge? How good is my picture? These questions helped create a paradox which plagued philosophers and scientists for over 2000 years.

How do you judge the accuracy of your picture? If you take a second picture, you have the same problem you had with the first. How do you take a picture of the original that's not a picture, a copy, a representation? It is impossible to experience something prior to its being experienced. You can only check your picture against new pictures or the pictures of other observers. As von Glasersfeld notes, the history of Western philosophy is the history of brilliant failures — philosophical systems which have failed to solve this problem.

A RECENT HISTORY OF OBJECTIVITY

Contemporary western culture glorifies knowledge and truth. Scientists, our new high priests of knowledge, are "our capable and mysterious liaison with reality, our ambassadors of wisdom."[8]

Prior to the 16th century a different conceptual apparatus was used to view reality. For 1500 years men knew God had made man in his own image and placed him on the stationary planet earth, the center of God's living, spiritual universe. Reality was hierarchical, "starting with God at the top and descending through the angels, human beings, and animals to the ever lower life forms."[9] All human action was explained teleologically, i.e., as taking place for the greater glory of God. Medieval science, for the most part a branch of Christian philosophy, sought to understand the meaning and significance of observed phenomena. Unlike their modern contemporaries, medieval scientists did not try to predict and control nature.[10]

In 1543 the medieval concept of reality began to unravel. Nicolaus Copernicus dared to assert that the earth moved on its axis and revolved around the sun. Following in his footsteps, Kepler and Galileo supplied additional evidence to support these revolutionary claims, speeding the overturn of Ptolemy's 1600-year-old geocentric universe. Man no longer lived in the center of the universe.

With this shift in thinking, reality took on a new appearance. Philosophers and scientists, who no longer assumed the great book of nature was written in biblical language, claimed nature's true language was mathematical. Galileo swept away the ideas of scholastic substances and teleological explanations, arguing that physical entities are composed of indestructible atoms, possessing mathematical qualities, and that atoms move in an infinite homogeneous space and time whose processes could be formulated mathematically. The real world is mathematical. "In short, all that mattered was matter."[11]

Galileo's spiritless world view was expanded and formalized by the philosopher and mathematician, René Descartes, who reduced the workings of nature to a geometric system. As Capra[12] states,

> At the age of twenty-three, Descartes experienced an illuminating vision that was to shape his entire life. After several hours of intense concentration, during which he reviewed systematically all the knowledge he had accumulated, he perceived, in a sudden flash of intuition, the "foundations of a marvelous science" which promised the unification of all knowledge. . . . In his vision Descartes perceived how he could realize this plan. He saw a method that would allow him to construct a complete science of nature about which he could have absolute certainty; a science based on mathematics, on self-evident first principles.

Descartes' ambition was reflected in the title of his most famous work, *Discourse on the Method of Rightly Conducting One's Reason and Searching For Truth in the Sciences.*

Descartes' "Cogito ergo sum" made the mind more certain for him than matter and led him to conclude that the two were separate and fundamentally different. Thus, he asserted that there is nothing included in the body that belongs to the mind, and nothing included in the mind that belongs to the body. This separation of mind and body has come to be known as Cartesian dualism.

Descartes' dualism allowed him to overcome several problems. First, as a religious man, he believed in the immortality of his soul. Dualism allowed him to reconcile his mechanical world view with his belief in God and the salvation of his soul. Second, he circumvented the problems of ambiguity associated with sense data. For hundreds of years, philosophers knew that sense data could be illusory or distorted. Rationalistic systems such as mathematics sidestep the uncertainty problem by limiting themselves to the logical domain. To wit, given the laws of addition, a logical system, two plus two must always equal four. Descartes' system would deduce the laws of matter.

Descartes' world of matter was a perfect machine, whose properties could be described and predicted mathematically. Descartes claimed that matter had only primary qualities—number, figure, size, position, and motion. Like his scientific contemporaries, he believed that primary qualities were properties of the real world, independent of observation.

The properties of mind were imagining, thinking, wishing, and other higher mental functions. "The mind was not located in space nor were its operations subject to mechanical laws. A person therefore lives through two collateral histories, one consisting of what happens in and to his body, the other consisting of what happens in and to his mind. The first is public, the second private. The events of the first history are events in the physical world; those in the second are events in the mental world."[13]

As a religious man, Descartes assumed God had created both substances. Once God had created the world of matter, however, man could discover God's original blueprint deductively, independent of sense experience, the way mathematical systems are deduced.

The mind-body split continues to plague scientists who study cognition and the nature of matter. As the physicist Werner Heisenberg comments, "This partition (Cartesian dualism) has penetrated deeply into the human mind during the three centuries that followed Descartes and it will take a long time for it to be replaced by a really different attitude toward the problem of reality."[14]

However, these problems took years to surface. In the immediate chain of historical events, Descartes' work set the stage for the mechanics of Sir Isaac Newton, the crown prince of classical science. Newton reduced Descartes' mechanistic universe of matter to three laws of motion and the law of gravity. His calculus depicted the material world as soulless, purposeless, lumps of matter moving in a coordinate system of absolute time and space.

As Rapoport[15] notes, the mathematics of classical science gave physics a powerful tool for understanding nature, providing a common denominator for understanding such apparently diverse phenomena as mechanics, light, sound, heat, electricity, and magnetism.

However, unlike Descartes, who limited himself to deduction, Newton, an empiricist, insisted that all deductions, no matter how rigorous, be confirmed with observation. Proving successful, Newton's mechanistic world view began to permeate western consciousness, touching every branch of human learning. Popularizers, by the hundreds, brought Newtonian wisdom to the general public. Thus, proclaimed the French social philosopher, Saint Simon, "Universal gravity is the sole cause of all physical and moral phenomena." The philosopher and mathematician d'Alembert[16] summarizes the impact of Newtonian thinking:

> Natural science from day to day accumulates new riches. . . . The true system of the world has been recognized. . . . In short, from the earth to Saturn, from the history of the heavens to that of insects, natural philosophy has been revolutionized; and nearly all other fields of knowledge have assumed new forms. . . . Spreading throughout nature in all directions, this fermentation has swept with a sort of violence everything before it which stood in its way, like a river which has burst its dams. . . . Thus, from the principles of secular science to the foundations of the religious revelations, from metaphysics to matters of taste, from music to morals, from the scholastic disputes of theologians to matters of commerce, from natural law to the arbitrary law of nations. . . . Everything has been discussed, analyzed or at least mentioned.

The scientific conception of reality which emerged in the 17th century is, in large part, responsible for our love affair with causality. "Newton gave the world the first rigorous formulation of the doctrine of causality. Most simply, the doctrine asserts that the same causes generate the same effects." The causal doctrine asserts that "the evolution of every physical system is controlled by rigorous laws. These, taken with the initial state of the system (assumed to be isolated), determine without ambiguity all future states and also all past states. The entire history of the system throughout time is thus determined by the laws and by the initial state."[17]

The doctrine of causality appeared to fulfill man's perennial search for certainty and objectivity. The philosophers and scientists of the 16th and 17th century thought they had circumvented, if not resolved, the problem of objectivity. Their method required two factors:

First, they assumed that nature operates without will or purpose, like a giant clockwork, independent of man and God. When the Emperor Napoleon asked Laplace, the French mathematican and astronomer, how God fit into his system, Laplace replied, "I have no need of that hypothesis." Or, as Robert J. Oppenheimer explains, "The giant machine (the Newtonian universe) was objective in the sense that no human act or intervention qualified its behavior." This same idea is expressed from a slightly different angle by Matson,[18] who writes, "Through the inexorable reduction of all knowable reality to the dimensions of objective mechanism, the gap between the knower and the known, between objective and subjective world, came to be the measure of the distance between appearance and reality."

Second, they developed procedures for *objectifying* observation to exclude human bias or render it inconsequential — the scientific method.

Although relativity theory and quantum mechanics have radically altered the physicist's view of reality, this shift has not touched the average person. Equally if not more important, many scientists have also failed to revise their thinking about reality and the nature of scientific work. Thus, most people see the world like 17th century scientists, assuming that it's possible to have objectivity and to know reality.

TRUTH, UNDERSTANDING, AND REALITY

Our 17th century mentality manifests itself in daily life. If this last statement sounds outlandish, stop and consider: Have you recently repaired some mechanical device, gathered data about the stock market, settled a dispute, checked your child's homework, or sat on a jury? Or, perhaps you earn your living testing new drugs, designing computers, practicing law, or investigating insurance claims? These activities and countless others require gathering data or information — not just any data, but data that are correct or accurate, i.e., that are true.

The search for objectivity and truth goes by many names. In the language of the marketplace, we ask for *the whole picture*, *the bottom line*, or *the facts*. The more scientifically minded speak of *accounting for the variance, establishing reliable and valid data, making accurate predictions*, and *validating hypotheses*.

Oversimplified, truth-seeking is like police work. Suppose a policeman suspects that Jones, an ex-convict, sells illegal drugs. After convincing a judge to grant him a search warrant, the policeman enters Jones' apartment and finds a pound of heroin and the paraphernalia to dilute it. The policeman has uncovered or, we might say, *discovered* the physical evidence that matches his belief. Reality has confirmed the policeman's picture of the world.

This, in brief, is how we assume objective knowledge is established, by matching something in the mind with something that we believe exists independently of us in the world of matter.

Continuously seeking direct confirmation for *our* thoughts and perceptions is impractical. Most of us do not have the time, money, skill, or resources. So we rely on what others tell us is true. We validate or modify our ideas and perceptions by *matching* them with the perceptions of others. Of course, we never know what goes on in other people's heads. So it might be more accurate to say that we match our perceptions against what other people *say* about their own.

Sometimes, we ask other people to tell us how things really are by reading their books. The book contains what others *say* are the facts. So the book becomes our source of truth, i.e., Reality. The book's authority depends on the author's procedures. Claims derived by scientific procedures have our highest esteem. Thus, we are more likely to believe the reports of an independent testing laboratory than the manufacturer's brochure.

When relying on our own senses, if we doubt input from one sensory input we check it with another. Confirming reality by matching two sensory inputs is dramatically demonstrated in the screen version of Alexander Dumas's classic tale, *The Count of Monte Cristo*. Durante, the story's hero, finds himself agonizing for the company of another person after many years of unjust, solitary confinement. One day a large stone in his prison cell begins to move and out crawls an old, bedraggled-looking man. Dumbfounded and speechless, Durante cannot believe his eyes. Initially, his visitor stands motionless. Durante must find out if he is hallucinating. He walks toward his perceived visitor, wide-eyed, holding his breath. Then, when in half an arm's distance of him, he stops and slowly touches the man's hair and face. After Durante has made this tactile connection, the expression on his face undergoes a metamorphosis. Wrapping his arms around the visitor, he heartily embraces him and begins crying tears of joy. "I was afraid you weren't real," says Durante. By correlating his sense of touch and vision, Durante believed he confirmed his reality.

However, we can not use one sense modality to confirm another and thus confirm objective reality. The eye cannot hear; the ear can not see. We can only correlate one sense experience with another. "As different as most philosophical, scientific, social, ideological or individual world images may be from one another," writes Watzlawick, "they still have one thing in common: the basic assumption that a reality exists and that certain theories, ideologies or personal convictions reflect it (match it) more correctly than others."[19]

CONSTRUCTIVISM

Scientists rarely challenge the assumption that reality exists independently of the observer. To do so, they must risk being labeled as odd or as seeking publicity. A growing number of renowned scholars and scientists, however, feel intellectually and emotionally compelled to take this risk. Known as constructivists, their ranks include anthropologist Gregory Bateson, psychologist-philosopher Ernst von Glasersfeld, psychologists Jean Piaget and Paul Watzlawick, biologists Humberto Maturana and Francisco Varela, neurophysiologist Warren McCulloch, physicist Erwin Schrodinger, and, of course, Heinz von Foerster. Von Foerster—

cybernetician, mathematician, physicist, and philosopher — claims that we CONSTRUCT or INVENT reality rather than discover it. He suggests that we fool ourselves by first dividing our world into two realities — the subjective world of our experience, and the so-called objective world of Reality — and then predicating our *understanding* on matching our experience with a world we assume exists independently of us.

When first contemplated, the notion of a constructed reality seems unfathomable and absurd. All is not chaos; the world has order. It exists! What could be more obvious? Von Foerster's constructed reality undermines our basis for obtaining knowledge. Does he think we simply invent reality by making it up in our heads? Is constructivism just another version of David Hume's solipsism?

No. Von Foerster is not a solipsist. He does not think we simply imagine the world. He does not deny reality. Like the rest of us, he dodges fast moving cars headed in his direction and does not attempt to walk through walls. Rather, as Rolf Breuer[20] explains, von Foerster maintains that " . . . the given 'objectivity' of the world is apparent and that it is incorrect to assume that biologists, psychologists, anthropologists, or physicists discover reality and represent it through description or formalism." Von Foerster argues that we have no basis for using "objectivity" to validate scientific arguments. Our belief in objectivity impedes scientific progress, especially our understanding of ourselves.

This is the key point in constructivism. If we begin with assuming objective reality, it determines our explanations of the observer. By rejecting objectivity, constructivists are not embracing solipsism. They reject the illusion of alternatives between an objective reality and solipsism. In this respect, their scientific endeavors are unique. Scientists are all too familiar with this problem. As physicist Max Planck[21] notes:

1) There is a real world which exists independently of our act of knowing.
2) The real outer world is not directly knowable.

The physicist D'Abro[22] argues that "the first of these statements cannot be proved or disproved by either *a priori* arguments or experiment; the stand of the solipsist is unassailable. For pragmatic reasons, however, the independent existence of the outer world must be granted."

"No," say von Foerster and Maturana. "We will not make that pragmatic assumption." They wish to avoid the kind of thinking found in the December 1984 issue of *Scientific American*, in which Cooper and Shepard,[23] in their article, "Turning Something Over in the Mind," state, "Our results confirm empirically what is subjectively apparent: that the mind can model physical processes, subjecting them to the geometric constraints that hold in the external world." Their starting point is the physical constraints in the *external world*. Their research aims to explain how the mind recreates what exists independently of it. But how do these writers know what physical constraints exist in reality prior to being known by an observer with a functioning nervous system? Their research, like most research on mentation, begs the question.

Constructivists argue that we *should not assume the independent existence of the outer world to explain the observer*.

A CLOSER LOOK AT OBJECTIVITY

What can the senses tell us about the world? This is no trivial problem. Science "endorses an epistemology (theory of knowledge) called empiricism. This epistemology is allegedly distinguished from several others (e.g., rationalism, mysticism) by the fact that it makes sense experience the ultimate source of knowledge. For the empiricist, all genuine knowledge must derive from or ultimately relate to sense data."[24] But the senses cannot give us perceptual certainty.

Traditional science attempts to control observer bias by excluding the observer. This position can be traced back to Galileo, who wrote, "I think that these tastes, colors, etc. . . . are nothing else than mere names, but hold residency solely in the sensitive body; so that if the animal(man) were removed, every such quality would be abolished or annihilated."[25] As stated earlier, the removal is accomplished with language.

The general rationale for objectivity is as follows: If a scientific explanation is valid, any qualified scientist, given the time, money and equipment, can reproduce the experiment and observe the same findings. "Scientific findings" are said to be independent of the person who does the scientific work. If replicable, the scientific community concludes that the findings represent a *discovery* about reality rather than a construction by the observer. The first scientist to make them public is said to have *discovered* them, e.g., Sir Isaac Newton discovered gravity. (The reader may note how natural the word *finding* appears in the context of this paragraph. However, this term "finding" conceals a metaphysical assumption that things can be found that exist independently of observers.)

While common sense suggests that the scientific method must control individual bias, a problem arises when we ask if a community of observers can be objective. Sharing agreements among observer-scientists does not prove that their sense data are objective, i.e., independent of observers. The entire proposition is absurd. How can you have science without observers? There would be nothing to observe!

Scientists will admit that scientific truths are at best consensually valid, but as D'Abro[26] explains, scientists assume objectivity for pragmatic reasons. Thus, we have "agreements" about explanations, called "scientific explanations." But scientists and laymen believe that objectivity validates the truthfulness of observations and explanations. This last point warrants further discussion. Scientific explanations use the object, existing independently of the observer, as the basis for their explanation. Surely this is a contradiction. How can that which cannot be known, the thing in itself, be used to validate an explanation!

Thus, we can distinguish two epistemologies: the epistemology of the observed system, endorsed by traditional science, and the epistemology of the observer, endorsed by the constructivists. Traditional scientists embrace an epistemology that argues that reality can be *confirmed* by matching our inner and outer worlds. Constructivists, embracing an epistemology of correlation, argue that our belief in objective reality arises from the *correlation* of our sense experience. I can see an object, I touch an object; therefore, I can correlate my experience of it and operate with it. If I correlate my experience of a pencil, I can write with it.

CONFIRMATION AND CORRELATION

The constructivists challenge the idea that we match experience to reality. They argue that we need not assume "objectivity" to do science. No findings exist independently of observers. Observing systems can only correlate their sense experiences with themselves and each other. "All we have are correlations," says von Foerster. "I see the pencil and I hold the pencil; I can correlate my experience of the pencil and use it. . . . There is a deep hiatus that separates *the* school of thought (about reality) from *a* school of thought, in which the distinct concepts of 'confirmation' and 'correlation,' respectively, are taken as explanatory paradigms for perceptions. To wit, *the* school says my sensation of touch is *confirmation* for my visual sensation that 'here is a table.' *A* school says my sensation of touch, in *correlation* with my visual sensation, generates an experience that I may describe as 'here is a table.'"[27]

As stated earlier, we cannot see what we hear or hear what we see. These are only inferences arising from correlating two sensory modalities. Stereoscopic vision provides another example of how we mistake confirmation for correlation. We do not confirm what we see with the left eye with what we see with the right eye, nor is the converse true. Each eye presents us with a different picture. Correlating these two pictures, we construct something new, the perception of depth.

STUDYING PERCEPTION

It is no mere accident that many constructivists challenge objectivity. Their studies in perception forced them to confront the issue of perceptual uncertainty. Scientists investigating phenomena other than cognition can sidestep perceptual uncertainty by assuming that when experimenter bias is adequately controlled, the senses report objective data about a *real* world. This position will not work when studying perception.

For example, if a scientist studies vision, how does he think about the object his subject views? In what domain does he claim the object exists — in the perceptual domain shared by him and the subject or in the domain of reality, independent of subject and scientist?

A student of perception, working like a traditional scientist, would exclude himself from his observations, linguistically relegating the objects in his experiments to the domain of Reality — with a capital R. He might design an experiment where the subject looks at a colored ball. He then performs experiments to explain how the subject can see it. Assuming the ball's *objective existence*, he attempts to explain how the subject sees it, i.e., how the subject's psychophysiological apparatus represents the ball in the subject's phenomenological experience. In other words, he explains how the subject perceives (grasps) objective reality. He assumes, *a priori*, that objects exist in the world, a metaphysical assumption. Is the purpose of his experiment to learn how we perceive objective reality or to learn about perception? Constructivists argue that the two are different. Observer (experimenter) and observed system (subject) may agree that they perceive the ball, but this does not mean it exists independently of them.

This subtle but most important point pervades the literature on perception and the brain. In his best-selling book *The Brain*, Richard Restak writes, "If you open up a television circuit from a camera to screen, nowhere will you find a miniaturized image of the world. And if we crack the skull to examine a brain, all we discover inside is a pinkish organ with the texture of an avocado. In both cases objects in the environment are not actually taken up into the television or the nervous system, but they are transformed instead into symbolic representations: glowing dots on the TV screen, or actively functioning neurons within our brains."[28] Implicit in Restak's description is the assumption that objects exist, independent of observers who transform them into symbolic representations.

How do scientists account for their own perceptual capacity to observe subjects? This question touches the central problem nagging students of perception for almost 100 years, *the problem of undifferentiated encoding.*

UNDIFFERENTIATED ENCODING

In 1860, Johannes Mueller formulated the principle of specific nervous energies. He noted that whatever you do to the eye, however you excite the rods and cones, the eye will always produce the sensation of light. For instance, a blow to the eye will produce a sensation of light, i.e., we see stars. This principle holds for all the sense modalities.

If we translate Mueller's principle of specific nervous energies into modern language, it tells us that it is not the stimulatory agent that produces the sensation we experience; it is the nervous system. No matter what stimulus we present a particular sensor — eye, ear, nose, etc. — it will always produce an experience of that sense modality.

We can restate this notion one more time as the principle of undifferentiated encoding: Our sensors only encode HOW MUCH stimulation they receive, NOT WHAT CAUSES THE STIMULATION. Thus, our sensors, our empirical link with reality, do not encode what stimulates them to fire. "How do we perceive such a rich world, full of sights, sounds, smells and colors?" asks von Foerster. Physicist Sir Arthur Eddington puts it this way:

> Consider how our supposed acquaintance with a lump of matter is attained. Some influence from it plays on the extremity of a nerve starting a series of physical and chemical changes which are propagated along the nerve to a brain cell; there a mystery happens, and an image of sensation arises in the mind which cannot purport to resemble the stimulus that excites it. Everything known about the material world must in one way or another have been inferred from the stimuli transmitted. . . . It is an astonishing feat of deciphering that we should have been able to infer an orderly scheme of natural knowledge from such indirect communication.[29]

Imagine what happens when a traditional scientist, trying to be objective by separating himself from his observation, investigates the perception of pressure. Figure 1 shows two eyes. One eye represents the experimenter, the observing system; the other eye represents the subject or the observed system. A mechanical sensor connects the subject's touch receptor, drawn in the shape of a pear, to meter (F), which measures how often the subject's pressure sensor fires. Meter (P) measures the pressure applied to the subject's body.

The experimenter applies pressure to the subject's skin as he views his two meters. Correlating the reading from the two meters, he validates that he is applying pressure to the subject's touch receptor. He might ask the subject, "What do you experience?" "Pressure," says the subject, appearing to confirm the observer's own conclusion. Here we have the matching principle in action. The observer matches his meters to each other and the subject's report.

The subject cannot see the experimenter applying pressure. Nor can he see the meters which measure pressure and the rate his sensor fires. But the subject experiences pressure. How does he know this?

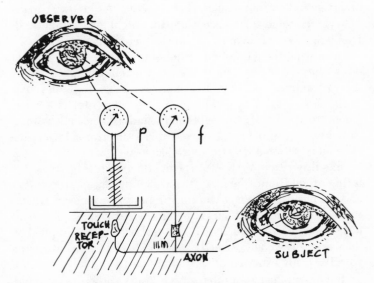

FIGURE 1. Observed and Observing Systems.

If the experimenter replicates the experiment with heat or something cold like ice, the subject's sensor, attached to a similar meter, will only show how often it fires, not what is perturbing it. The subject does not have or need a meter. He simply senses pressure, or heat, or cold. How does this experience come about? As Eddington asked, how does the subject create this experience from a series of nerve impulses which only encode the amount of stimulation, not what is stimulating them?

The experimenter *verifies* the subject's experience of pressure by matching observations from his two meters. One shows pressure; the other, the rate at which the sensor fires. He then hypothesizes: "I must have my probe in a touch receptor; my meters correlate perfectly." The experimenter overlooks how the subject knew pressure was applied to his arm. The subject could not see the pressure meter or what the experimenter did to his arm. The subject perceived pressure, yet his nervous system only encodes the degree of stimulation, not *what* perturbs it. The sensor's message contains nothing about pressure. How do we turn 80 millivolt pulses of electrical current traveling through our nervous system into the experience of pressure or vision or whatever? If the observer used an epistemology that accounted for his own capacity to perceive and experience, this point might not go unnoticed. He might ask, "How am I capable of perceiving?"

Answering these questions requires giving up the belief that our sensors — our eyes, our ears, etc. — when uncontaminated by emotion and motive, work like cameras and microphones, passively cabling data to the brain, which, like a television set, reconverts the signals into sights and sounds produced by reality.

In short, the problem can be revealed as an error in logic. Like all good traditional scientists we make logical inferences, i.e., A implies B, written $A \rightarrow B$. If A is true, then B must be true. If A is false, then B must be false. If a weight is placed on our arm and our nervous system is working properly, we have visual and tactile sensations. We then say to ourselves or others, "I see and feel the world. My sensations(B) are 'real perceptions' implied by the world (the weight), which I know exists." Thus we have A(the world) $\rightarrow$ B(my experience).

But as von Foerster protests, "It is just the other way around.

The implication is that I infer the weight because I have particular sensations. From my sensations I make an inference about the world." In the logical equation $A \rightarrow B$, A is our experience; B is our inference of a reality. Of course, this reverses our usual thinking about ourselves and the world.

A CLOSER LOOK AT THE OBSERVER

Reality supposedly contains objects that either are stationary or change their position in space. Though some objects, like human beings, have a changeable structure, they are perceived as having sameness and continuity. Our structure is constantly changing, but our friends and relatives recognize us as the same persons. "What do we mean by change?" asks von Foerster. "Despite change in appearance of the an object, as when a cube is rotated or a person turns around, we take it to be the same object."[30] How does change apply to a "tree growing, or when we meet an old school mate after a decade or two? Are they different or are they the same?"[31] Perceiving reality depends on distinguishing between invariance and change.

Newborns do not have object constancy, the capacity to distinguish stable objects. They cannot compute *equivalence*, a logical operation that must be performed to perceive an object which changes its structure or position in space as the same object. Developmental studies of children, conducted by the Swiss psychologist Jean Piaget, show that we learn to perceive object constancy. It takes about 18 months; Piaget calls this type of learning "sensorimotor intelligence." It "involves the establishment of relationships and correspondences (functions) and classification of schemes (cf. the logic of classes); in structures of ordering and assembling that constitute a substructure for the future operations of thought." Sensorimotor intelligence "organizes reality by constructing broad categories of action which are the schemes of the permanent object, space, time, causality. . . . "[32]

For instance, sit down with a five-year-old child and lay out five pennies in a row on the top of a table. Then give the child five pennies and ask him to make a row matching your own. This the child can do easily. A five-year-old child can also tell you that

each row has the same number of pennies. If, however, you increase the space between the pennies in one of the rows and then
ask him which row contains more pennies, a five-year-old child
will say the longer row has more pennies than the shorter row.
Elkind notes that the same exercise with a seven-year-old has a
different outcome. "In the first place the child regards the question as rather stupid and replies that of course the two rows have
the same number of pennies since nothing was added or taken away
and spreading them apart does not alter their number. The older
child takes as self-evident, or *a priori*, what only a few years ago
he did not know existed. *Once a concept is constructed, it is immediately externalized so that it appears to the subject as a perceptually given property of the object and independent of the
subject's own mental activity. The tendency of mental activities
to become automatized and for their results to be perceived as
external to the subject is what leads to the conviction that there
is a reality independent of thought.*"[33]

Piaget's work suggests that we reevaluate the meaning of fac-
tual knowledge. *Webster's New World Dictionary*[34] defines a fact
as "2. A thing that has really happened or that is really true; 3.
the state of things as they really are, reality; actuality, truth;
fact as distinguished [from fancy]." If we dig a little deeper
however, by consulting the *American Heritage Dictionary*,[35] we
find the word fact is derived from the Latin root *facere*, which
means to do or to make. *Facere* is the Latin root in such words
as factor, fashion, artifact, benefactor, edifice, infect, justify,
modify, nullify, perfect, profit, rectify, etc.

On his 81st birthday, in a debate with the linguist Noam
Chomsky, Piaget stated: "Fifty years of experience have taught
us that knowledge does not result from a mere recording of observations without a structuring activity on the part of the subject."[36]
Thus, there are no 'pure facts.' A fact is interpreted from the moment of its observation.

Constructivist Ernst von Glasersfeld,[37] sharing Piaget's concept of cognition, writes, "Radical constructivism maintains . . .
that the operations by means of which we assemble our experiential world can be explored, and that an awareness of this oper-

ating . . . can help us do it differently and, perhaps, better." The remainder of this book will examine those operations.

WHAT ABOUT TECHNOLOGICAL PROGRESS?

The reader may wonder how constructivists reconcile their refutation of objectivity with our culture's tremendous technological advances, which are directly attributable to scientific discoveries.

Constructivists argue that technological advances show "one" of many possible ways to bring about a result or make predictions. A proven scientific theory is a successful means for reaching a goal.

Von Glasersfeld explains that 1) knowledge, particularly scientific knowledge, is useful if it allows us to predict, i.e., to bring about or avoid certain phenomena. 2) When knowledge no longer serves that purpose it becomes questionable and eventually devalued. 3) Von Glasersfeld concludes, "Any cognitive structure [he is referring to a theory or model] that serves its purpose in our time, therefore, proves no more or no less than that—namely, given the circumstances we have experienced (and determined *by* experiencing them), it has done what was expected of it. Logically, this gives us no clue as to how the *objective* world might be; it merely means we know one viable way to a goal that we have chosen under specific circumstances in our experiential world. It tells us nothing—and cannot tell us anything—about how many other ways there might be or how that experience that we consider the goal might be connected to the world beyond our experience."

"The metaphysical realist," continues von Glasersfeld,[38] "looks for knowledge in the same way as you might look for paint to match the color that is already on the wall. . . . Philosophers and scientists, operating on the matching principle, try to match systems of relationships or structures with 'nature.'"(The term nature is a synonym for Reality.)

"If, on the other hand," continues von Glasersfeld, "we say that something 'fits,' we have in mind a different relation. A key fits if it opens the lock. It describes the capacity of the key, not the lock. Thanks to professional burglars we know only too well there are many keys that are shaped quite differently from our own that open the lock."

THEORY OF THE OBSERVER

Von Foerster's work attempts to explain the observer. Constructivists are more concerned with *how* we know than with *what* we know. How do we cognize? What does it means to dwell in "object" language?

Francisco Varela describes von Foerster's ideas as a framework for understanding cognition in which the descriptions of the observer and that which is observed are "inextricably" connected. "The study of first order systems (those we study) and the study of second order systems (we the observers) are reflected in such descriptions. This mutually specifying pair, in all its details, constitutes a space where cognition can be properly understood."[39] Thus, the observer must account for himself in his observations.

How does the observer account for himself? This is not an easy notion to summarize. Von Foerster introduces the problem with the following puzzle.

"THIS SENTENCE HAS _____ LETTERS."

He asks us to insert the missing word, i.e., spell out the name of a number which accurately accounts for all the letters in the sentence, including the letters in the missing word.

Only certain numbers solve the problem. The words "ten" or "fifty" will not work. If you insert the word "thirty-one," however, you will find that the sentence, including your answer, contains 31 letters. But there is another correct answer! To solve this problem, the answer must take itself into account! It must include the number of its own letters. The reader is encouraged to stop reading and find the second correct solution.

The puzzle illustrates a subtle yet extremely important point — *there is more than one correct answer to this problem.* Traditional science seeks *necessary* answers to its problems, i.e., solutions having one and only one answer. Scientists rely heavily on mathematics, a system constructed to generate necessary answers to its questions. If we ask how much is two times three, the answer must be six. Von Forester's sentence is unique; it has two correct answers.

Von Foerster's puzzle reveals one consequence of constructivism — the loss of certainty! Necessary answers generate certainty. A subject-dependent science which permits and encourages the observer to include himself in his observations cannot generate necessary answers. Constructivists argue that nothing is really lost here. We never had certainty to begin with. We can invent keys that unlock our problems, but these inventions only tell us about the key, not about the lock. Several keys unlock von Foerster's puzzle. Although certainty is lost, choice increases.

SUMMARY

I shall use the following quote from von Foerster's paper, "Notes on an Epistemology for Living Things,"[40] to summarize my remarks on objectivity:

> While in the first quarter of this century physicists and cosmologists were forced to revise the basic notions that govern the natural sciences, in the last quarter of this century biologists will force a revision of the basic notions that govern science itself. By the early 20th century it was clear that the classical concept of an "ultimate science," a science which purported an objective description of the world in which there are no subjects (a "subjectless universe"), contains contradictions.
>
> To remove these contradictions science was forced to account for an "observer" (i.e., at least one subject). Here are two examples of this shift in scientific thinking: 1) observations are not absolute but relative to the observer's point of view (i.e., his coordinate system — Einstein's theory of relativity); 2) observations affect the observed so as to obliterate the observer's

hope of prediction (i.e., his uncertainty is absolute —
Heisenberg's uncertainty principle).

Given these changes in scientific thinking, we are
now in the possession of the truism that a description
(of the universe) implies one who describes (observes
it). What we need now is a description of the "describer" or, in other words, we need a theory of the
observer. Since only living organisms qualify as observers, it appears that this task falls to the biologist.
But the biologist is also a living being, which means
that in his theory he has to account not only for himself but also for his writing the theory. This is a new
state of affairs in scientific discourse, for in line with
the traditional viewpoint which separates the observer
from his observations, reference to this discourse was
carefully avoided. This separation was not done because of eccentricity or folly. Scientists obeyed this
rule of separation because, under certain circumstances,
when the observer included himself in his description
(observations) it led to paradox, like the paradox one
finds in the statement, "I am a liar."

In the meantime, however, it has become increasingly clear that this narrow restriction, i.e., excluding
the observer, not only creates ethical problems associated with scientific activity, but cripples the study
of life in its full context from molecular to social or-
ganizations. Life cannot be studied *in vitro*; one has
to explore it *in vivo*. In contrast to the classical problem of scientific inquiry that postulates first a description-invariant "objective world" (as if there were such
a thing) and then attempts to describe it, we are now
challenged to develop a description-invariant "subjective world," that is, a world which includes the observer. *This is the problem.*

However, in accord with the classical tradition of
scientific inquiry, which perpetually asks "how?" rather than "what?" this task calls for an epistemology
of "How do we know?" rather than "What do we
know?"

2

The Difficulties
of Language

. . . language is itself the vehicle of thought.[1]

Thinking and language belong together. A child learns
a language in such way that it suddenly begins to
think in it.[2]

— Ludwig Wittgenstein

There is no stage in a child's development, notes Wittgenstein,[3] when language is used to communicate but not to think. Grammar and syntax are rules for thinking, which philosophers call epistemology. Gregory Bateson explains "in the West our language presents us with a linear causal view of the world. Language continually asserts by the syntax of subject and predicate that 'things' somehow 'have' qualities and attributes."[4]

Consider this hypothetical example: Four-year-old Mark and his two-year-old sister, Pat, play in the family room while their mother works in the kitchen. Mother hears Pat cry and rushes in to comfort her. As she enters, Mark says, "I didn't touch her."

By the tender age of four, Mark has assimilated an important rule of his culture's epistemology. Remarking "I didn't touch her," he proclaims his innocence by taking the Newtonian position on causality. He unwittingly argues that without touching her, he could not have transmitted a force or impact which caused Pat to cry. There is no causal connection between his own behavior and his sister's distress.

Causality, however, is only one example of how language determines our thinking. Language structures a variety of logical, descriptive, and explanatory devices we use to understand ourselves and reality. I have grouped von Foerster's comments under the following categories: re-presentation, nominalization, localization of function, logical syllogisms, paradox, causality, and explanations.

RE-PRESENTATION

By defining us as passive agents of perception, language hides how we participate in our sensory experience. For instance, everyone knows that light bulbs produce light, and it seems natural to speak of "turning on the lights" or "throwing the light switch." But does the bulb produce light? A physicist would say that electrons run through the bulb's filament and when it becomes hot enough, the filament emits electromagnetic waves which act on the rods and cones in the eye's retina. Under these conditions, if an observer is properly located and his nervous system functional, he experiences light. Blind people do not see light.

By defining light as a property of the light bulb, language simultaneously hides how we participate in our sensory experience, defining light as an objective property of the world, a property independent of the observer. This is also true for sound. We say (and think) that drawing a bow over a violin string makes sound. "No," contends von Foerster, "You're producing periodic variations of the air pressure which travel in space. If an ear, with a brain attached to it, happens to be in that same space, then we hear music. Nor does a campfire produce heat. When you sense an increase in average molecular velocity of the air space around you, you say, 'It's warm.'"

"The problem begins with the book of Genesis," says von Foerster. "There it says: 'God was floating over the waters and it was dark. God said, "There shall be light" and there was light.' But how could there be light? Nobody was there to see it. You can't have light without an observer. God may have said, 'There

shall be electromagnetic radiation of particular frequency band'
and there were electromagnetic radiations of that frequency band.
But ladies and gentlemen, this is so aesthetically displeasing, it
must be wrong. Here is what I think took place: And God was
floating over the waters and he said, '*Let there be vision*' and
there was light!"*

NOMINALIZATION

Nominalization denotes the linguistic process for turning verbs
into nouns. Thus, language allows us to convert actions or processes into things. Nominalization pathologically afflicts all Indo-
European languages by allowing us to create things out of the
thin air. We can say a horse gallops, but language also permits
us to say that a horse has a good gallop. Though grammatically
correct, this last sentence claims the horse possesses a gallop the
way he possesses horse shoes.

Nominalization occurs in many domains, including psychiatry. Language has lulled many psychotherapists into thinking of
behavior as a thing. Historically, psychiatrists labeled certain
aberrant behavior "schizophrenia," but before long they began
to call their patients schizophrenics and thought of them as having schizophrenia the way they might have a diseased liver. Some
practitioners became so enamored with their nominalizations
that they believed mental illness a palpable disease that could be
"cut out" with psychosurgery.

When we nominalize something, it becomes a commodity,
something to be bought and sold. As an educator, von Foerster
is particularly concerned with negative consequences of nominalizing "information" and "knowledge."

> The primordial and most proprietary processes in
> any man, and in fact any organism, namely "infor-
> mation" and "knowledge," are now persistently taken

---

*It is easy to misinterpret the statements about electromagnetic radiation to mean
that there is a reality independent of the observer which contains electromagnetic
radiation. Von Foerster uses the term "electromagnetic radiation" in the constructivist sense to describe a key which is useful to unlock problems.

as commodities, that is, as substance. Information is, of course, the process by which knowledge is acquired, and knowledge is the process that integrates past and present experiences to form new activities as nervous activity perceived either internally as thought and will or externally as speech and movement.

Neither of these processes can be "passed on" as we are told in phrases like "Universities are depositories of knowledge that can be passed on from generation to generation."[5]

Understandably, many students are disappointed by education systems that "confuse creating new processes with the dispensing of goods called 'knowledge,'" goods impossible to deliver.

Thinking about thinking is particularly susceptible to nominalization. We can say that people think; we can also say that they have thoughts. The word "thought," however, is a noun. Many nouns are "things," having substance and location. Assuming that a person "has thoughts," we soon try to find them. But can you find a thought? Many researchers believe that thinking, memory, imagination, and other mental functions are housed in specific areas of the brain, a theoretical viewpoint called *localization of function*.

LOCALIZATION OF FUNCTION

Von Foerster traces the genesis of this belief to 15th century anatomists who knew that personality and character traits correlated with the shape and protuberances of the skull. Figure 2A shows a map drawn by Reisch in 1503. Memory is housed on the left upper frontal lobe; other locations house cognition, fantasies, and imagination. Such maps exemplify guess work at its best, aided and abetted by our ability to nominalize. Later, phrenologists, like Redfield, mapped hundreds of locations onto the skull, each area supposedly representing a higher mental function (Figure 2B).

Using the face and the skull, Redfield claimed to have found no fewer than 186 localized functions. For example 149 is the

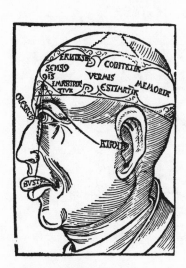

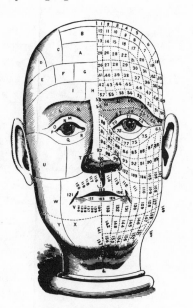

FIGURE 2A.
Phrenology Diagram,
Reisch — 1503

FIGURE 2B.
Phrenology Diagram,
Redfield — 1886

location of Republicanism; 148 Faithful Love; and 149A Responsibility.

"Do not assume localization of function ended in the Middle Ages," say von Foerster. "The search for localization of brain functions never seems to stop." In 1881, Exner (see Figure 3), a brilliant Austrian neurophysiologist, claimed to precisely map hundreds of cortical "centers." For many years, his work contributed to the misunderstanding of mental functions.

Observing that a brain lesion, from either a bullet wound or another injury, correlated with the loss of behavior or function, like the ability to speak, to see, or to walk, Exner mistakenly assumed that the location of these lesions must house the missing functions. Exner would not have made this mistake if he were aware of how he was nominalizing processes.

During one of von Foerster's talks a woman in the audience

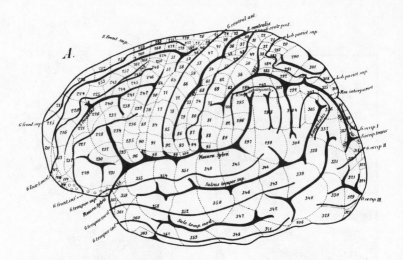

FIGURE 3. Localization of Function Based on Cortical Lesions, Exner, 1881

said, "You're arguing against localization of function but I had a personal experience that makes me believe in it. Recently my husband suffered a mild brain concussion. After regaining consciousness, he could not speak. Naturally, we became extremely concerned and rushed him to the hospital. The doctor found a small blood clot in his brain. After the clot was removed, he could speak again. Doesn't that prove that his speech center was impaired?" she asked.

"No," said von Foerster. "Your husband's blood clot does not prove his speech center was impaired. Reasoning this way involves a fundamental error in deduction. Damage to a particular area of the brain may correlate with a temporary or permanent loss of function. This does not prove localization of function. The brain functions as a whole system. Naturally, damage to one part of the system may lead to an impairment of function like speech or vision.

"Consider the following analogy. Suppose your car won't start. A mechanic finds the problem—a piece of dirt in the fuel line prevented gas from entering the carburetor. Would you conclude that the car's capacity for movement was localized at that spot? No, of course not! The localization of function argument suggests the car's ability to move is localized in the fuel line. That's ridiculous! The whole system determines the car's capacity for locomotion. Naturally, if the engine develops a problem because one of its parts breaks down, the car will not move! Attributing loss of function to the absence of brain tissue is a mistake. We are always dealing with a whole brain. An injured brain has a specific constraint, but it is still functioning as a *whole* brain.

"We must look at the entire system and avoid the temptation to look at one little corner of it or to treat it like a machine that can be disassembled so that each part can be understood separately. The system must be understood by looking at all the parts together."

Looking for memory is another attempt to localize brain functions, to nominalize mental processes. The search intensified when psychologists began using computer metaphors to understand the brain. Computer metaphors are understandably appealing. The computer's memory is finite, having a definite location. If you open a microcomputer's cabinet, you can see the "memory" chips. Von Foerster argues, "Computing machines do not have memories. That's the first mistake. Computers have storage systems. If you carelessly use this charming metaphor, you may begin asking, 'Can this machine write its memoirs?' Not the way they are designed today!"

Second, he demonstrates by *reductio absurdum* that our memories cannot function like storage devices in computers. A computer's data storage system (what is unfortunately called memory) is a giant filing system. Each file has an address. The computer retrieves data from a file by looking up the address, going to it, retrieving the data, and then displaying it on the monitor or using it for a computation. Naturally, it does this extremely fast. Von Foerster: "If our memory worked like a computer's data storage system, we would need a brain a mile in diameter, packed with nerve cells, to account for what we know." Even if we could retrieve data at the speed of light, he points out that with a system this large, it would take us ten years to recognize an object, a state of affairs extremely detrimental to our survival.

But there is an even stronger argument against assuming that memory is a data storage system. In a computer stored data are retrieved from storage based on a perfect match. Those readers who have used home computers may know how frustrating it can be to have the machine unable to find what they're looking for because they put in an extra white space between words or capitalized a letter. The computer is unforgiving when matching.

The question now arises: What happens when we want to remember something like finding our car in the parking lot? If our memory worked like the computer, we would never find our car because we never see things exactly the same way twice. There are multiple variables that go into computing a retinal image, and these are never exactly the same. If our memories worked like computer data storage systems, we would never find a match. Fortunately, memory works differently; thus we can recognize our car from many different angles, distances, and light conditions.

Around 1925, von Damerous, a brilliant young neurologist, demonstrated the logical fallacy of associating cortical lesions with the loss of brain functions. First he claimed that the capacity for stereoscopic vision (spatial vision) must be located in the left eye. If someone loses his left eye, he no longer has stereoscopic vision. Therefore, the left eye must house this function.

Von Damerous then argued that if you accept this conclusion, then you must also accept the same argument for the right eye. Because if the right eye is lost, one also loses the capacity for spatial vision. Thus, both arguments become equally ridiculous. "Once you see the fallacy in this reasoning," says von Foerster, "the argument for localizing brain functions falls to pieces."

Von Foerster cautions, "You probably think that nobody thinks along these lines today. Unfortunately, it never stops. I'm referring to the hemispherologists, the chaps who say, 'On the left side I have this, on the right I have that. And with my left hemisphere I kick the football; and with the right hemisphere I smell the flowers,' or some such thing. As a constructivist, let me make my position perfectly clear — the brain always functions as a whole, as a totality. Even injured, it is still a whole brain, a whole brain with an injury. A brain-injured person may function with specific constraints, manifesting certain deficiencies, but this in no way proves localization of function."

Additional evidence suggests that the brain functions as a whole system. If nerve cells deteriorate slowly enough, other parts of the brain compensate for them. Louis Pasteur, the great French chemist, remained professionally active until his death at age 73. He bequeathed his body to the Sorbonne medical school, whose physicians performed an autopsy on it. To their great surprise, they found that his left hemisphere, the side of the brain believed to house the capacities for logic and thinking, was almost totally consumed by a massive brain tumor. Pasteur's tumor grew slowly, permitting the healthy brain tissue to participate in functions usually operative in the left hemisphere. If brain functions were localized, compensation could not occur.

Summing up, the attempt to perceive brain function as localized arises from epistemological errors that can impede our understanding of cognition:

1) First, it nominalizes processes, suggesting that they are located in specific tissue of the cerebral cortex.

2) It implies that localized cortical areas are decoding centers for the senses and storage devices, reifying our belief in "objective" reality.

3) The localization of function argument suggests that the nervous system is an open system, that our sensory and motor systems are independent, a subject more closely examined in upcoming chapters.

4) Finally, and maybe most important, the localization of function argument avoids the primary problem of cognition, the principle of undifferentiated encoding. It fails to answer the question: Why do we have such a rich experience of the world when our sensors only encode the amount of stimulation they receive, not the nature of the perturbing stimulus?

LOGICAL SYLLOGISMS

The logical syllogism is a system of reasoning we use to make inferences. Rationalist philosophers used the syllogism to obtain knowledge. They believed the mind was endowed with *a priori* (innate) knowledge, ready-made principles and faculties, which can be discovered by correct reason. Plato called this innate knowledge "forms" or "ideas" which would include the concepts of number, difference, good, bad, right and wrong.

Around 300 B.C., Aristotle wrote the famous Organon, a Greek word meaning instrument. Using the syllogism, he defined 14 rules of reasoning for properly drawing conclusions from propositions. "It was said that conclusions reached by the syllogism satisfied three conditions; they were true, necessitated, and new."[6] In this context, a necessary conclusion means the only conclusion, i.e., there can be no other answer.

The syllogism was the rationalist's royal road to certainty. As Guillen[7] explains, "It is a rare person who does not prefer certainty over doubt in most matters and an even rarer person who can obtain it. It was as though certainty were a buried treasure, and we who so desire it have yet to find a map that can lead us to it. Around 300 B.C., mathematicians believed they had found such a map in the guiding principles of Aristotle's logic. Euclid followed those principles in proving the theorems of geometry (the study of shapes), which were hailed as models of certainty for 2000 years."

A syllogism is a three part argument. It contains: 1) a major premise; 2) a minor premise; and 3) a conclusion. As Pospesel[8] explains, "An argument is a set of statements, one of which (the conclusion) supposedly follows from the others (the premises). There are two types of syllogisms — deductive and inductive."

Deductive syllogisms

Most readers have some acquaintance with the famous deductive syllogism about Socrates. First, the major premise: *All men are mortal*. Second, the minor premise: *Socrates is a man*. Third, the conclusion: *Socrates is mortal!* The conclusion is inescapable; it is absolutely necessary.

"Is Socrates' mortality a property of Socrates?" asks von Foerster. "Hardly," he says. "It is a property of the syllogism." Once we declare all men mortal and define Socrates as a man, the syllogism's structure requires us to infer Socrates' mortality. This conclusion is a logical necessity of the syllogism, not a necessary fact about Socrates. Of course, a constructivist would argue that this is no great surprise. What is a syllogism but a logical device which we construct? Just as language fools us by putting light into the light bulb, the syllogism misleads us into attributing the observer's properties to the observed system. We unconsciously invent these properties with logic and assume we discover them in the systems we observe.

Von Foerster: "Let me draw your attention to the following points, starting with the first premise: All men are mortal. This means all men will die. Is this an absolute fact? This is merely an assumption. Obviously it's not a bad one, but it is still an assumption. We have some conflicting evidence. Look around you. We are all sitting here pretty much alive. Who is it that knows all men are mortal? I have no idea! If you consider this proposition from a probabilistic point of view, we can make the following argument. There are about 80 billion people that ever walked the face of the earth. On this planet, there are roughly 4 billion people alive at the moment, so there's about a 5% probability that you are immortal! Assuming that we will all die, who will report that all men are mortal? The entire proposition is ridiculous.

"We need to take a deeper look at these logical devices and the words of their propositions. We begin with the major premise, 'All men are mortal,' without concern for its semantics, as if the proposition were a universal truth. A more accurate way of casting this syllogism would be as follows: *If* all men were mortal and Socrates is a man, then Socrates *may be* mortal. Look what has happened. Something has disappeared. It's called certainty!"

Syllogistic reasoning permeates everyday thinking. By condensing the process, our syllogistic reasoning becomes invisible. For example, one marital partner confronts the other on his unacceptable behavior at a neighbor's cocktail party. The accused says, "Sorry, I must have had too much to drink." When the accused's statement is expanded to its full syllogistic form, it reads as follows: 1) major premise — people who are intoxicated do not mean what they say, 2) minor premise — "I was intoxicated"; 3) conclusion — "therefore, I didn't mean what I said!"

Here are two more examples, drawn from Howard Pospesel's delightful book on logic.[9] First: "A friend of mine who suffered from dizzy spells underwent tests by a neurosurgeon. When they met to discuss the results, the following conversation took place: Doctor: David, you have a benign tumor in your inner ear. It's called an acoustic neuroma. David: How can you be sure it's benign? Doctor: Acoustic neuromas are always benign.

Wishing to convey how often we use this logical device, Pospesel offers a second, more mundane example. The University of Miami Library has restrooms on each floor. The odd-numbered floors house the men's restrooms; the even-numbered floors house the women's restrooms. He writes, "One day recently, as I absentmindedly passed through the doorway of one of these rooms, I was gripped by the neurotic fear that I was walking into the wrong kind of restroom. The anxiety dissolved when I spotted a urinal."[10]

Once again we see the condensation of the logical syllogism. Pospesel's thinking, presented in a formalism, would read: "All restrooms with urinals are men's rooms. This room has a urinal. Therefore, it is a men's room." Luckily, he was not in a Stanford University dormitory, which has coed restrooms!

Inductive syllogisms

The inductive syllogism is the basis of natural science. When reasoning inductively, we infer the general case from what we know about specific cases. For example: Socrates is a man. Socrates is mortal, for indeed, he died! Therefore, all men are mortal. "This sounds utterly crazy," says von Foerster, "How can one reason like this? But this is exactly what we do when we make inductive inferences. Consider the inductive inference restated in its most abstract formulation: You examine something (a process or a thing) and observe that two properties — P1 and P2 — are always present in each specific case. Then you predict that in all future cases in which you find P1 you also will find P2."

You may predict that your bus will arrive on time because it has not been late for the past two months or that your car will start because it's new and has never had trouble starting. But eventually, you will be wrong. Inductive syllogisms only work up to a point. Errors will occur when making inductive inferences because the logical structure is inherently fallible. Challenging the belief in certainty, David Hume made this point quite dramatically when he argued that just because the sun has risen every morning does not permit us to assume that it will "necessarily" rise tomorrow. Thus, von Foerster argues that *necessity* and *chance* are properties of the observer's logical devices — not of the systems he observes. Necessity and chance arise from our rules of thought.

In sum:

1) NECESSITY → arises from the ability to make infallible deductions.
2) CHANCE → arises from the inability to make infallible inductions.

PARADOX AND SELF-REFERENCE

A paradox is a statement that is false when it is true and true when it is false. Paradox can occur whenever statements are self-referential. For instance: 1) This statement is false. 2) I am lying. 3) Please ignore this notice. 4) It is forbidden to forbid.

Each statement comments on itself. The moment you make self-referential statements the logicians will immediately protest, "You can't do that!" "But why not?" you might ask. "Because," say the logicians, "self-referential statements produce paradoxes. They contaminate logical systems!"

Why the logician's objection to paradox? The answer is quite simple. Logicians work with declarative statements called propositions. Over 2000 years ago, Aristotle taught that if a proposition makes sense, it *must be either true or false*. Each proposition must meet this criterion to qualify for membership in a scientific doctrine. Otherwise, it is unacceptable. Paradox renders a proposition's truth value indeterminable. Paradoxical statements or propositions are neither true nor false.

Do not think, however, that the objection to paradox is limited to philosophy. Scientists use propositions to make scientific explanations. Thus, science and philosophy share the same objection to paradox.

The etymological roots of paradox

The word paradox has two Greek roots: *Para* meaning "outside" and *doxein* meaning "to point, to show, to teach." So paradox means "outside of the teaching." "Orthodox" (from the Greek root *ortho* meaning straight) means the straightforward or insidé teachings. For thousands of years, the orthodox teaching was Aristotelian. The first people who made paradoxical statements challenged Aristotle's teaching.

Von Foerster humorously describes how, in the 6th century B.C., along came a chap from Crete. He traveled by boat to Athens, and on landing announced, "I am from the island of Crete and all Cretans are liars." This famous Cretan, Epimenidies, confused the Aristotelian logicians. "If you are from Crete, and you say all Cretans are liars, then you must have lied. Aha! But if you have lied, then you spoke the truth because you said all Cretans are liars. But when you spoke the truth, then you must have lied." The Aristotelians dealt with this sticky problem by ignoring it.

When the Christian Church began to represent "the teaching," anything taught outside its doctrine was labeled paradoxical. Those who rejected its teaching were considered paradoxical people. Between the first and second millennium, however, Aristotle was rediscovered, and philosophers and logicians once more considered his writings "the teaching." So the term paradox resumed its original meaning. People who publicly expressed ideas outside Church doctrine were given a new name—heretics. The

Greek root of heretics is *heiresis*, which means "choice." Heretics were people who kept their freedom of choice. The Church forbid choice. Those who insisted on choosing were burned at the stake.

The barber paradox

The barber story can clarify how a paradox works. Like all paradoxes, it contains a proposition which is true when it is false and false when it is true. The story is as follows:

In a little village lives a barber, who shaves only those villagers who do not shave themselves. If you live in the village and don't shave yourself, the barber will shave you. Of course, if you do shave yourself, the barber will not shave you.

Now, the question which generates the paradox: Should the barber shave himself? The logic used to think through this question might go like this: If the barber were to shave himself, he would be a "self-shaver," belonging to the class called "self-shavers." If this were the case, then he should *not* shave himself, because he only shaves people who *do not* shave themselves. But if he does not shave himself, he is not a self-shaver and should shave himself!

The conclusion of our syllogistic thinking oscillates as we try working our way through the paradox. For the past 2000 years paradox has given logicians and philosophers tremendous headaches. Aristotelians knew that a sensible proposition must be either true or false. Paradox confounds this rule. So what to do? The philosopher Bertrand Russell found an interesting solution called "The Theory of Logical Types."

Bertrand Russell and paradox

Bertrand Russell's involvement with the paradox began when he found a paradox in the work of Gottlob Frege. As Guillen[11] explains, " . . . in the late 1800s mathematicians embarked *en masse* on a program to do for arithmetic what Euclid had done for geometry. The general idea was to reformulate the hodge-podge of arithmetical results that had accumulated over the centuries into some kind of logical format." Declaring their faith in deductive reasoning, many mathematicians set themselves to the task, but Gottlob Frege was the first to declare that he had finished it. Guillen continues, "He had worked from 1893 to 1902 to derive hundreds of theorems of arithmetic from just a few assumptions, and the tangible results were a monumental two-volume treatise entitled *Grundgesetze der Arithmetik (Fundamental Laws of Arithmetic)*. His assumptions, like Euclid's, might be challenged, but his conclusions were drawn according to principles of deductive reasoning that were consistent, although technically not identical with Aristotle's."[12]

Frege was about to publish his second volume when Russell discovered a paradox, exactly like the paradox in the barber story, in his first volume. Russell's paradox has to do with logical classes and the logical elements the classes may contain. A class is a logical collection of objects that share a defined property. If one defines a class of books — all books past, present and future — one can logically separate all objects in the universe into two classes: those that have class membership and those that don't. If we allow a self-referential statement by asking if the class is a book, no paradox occurs. The class of books is not a book.

If a proposition states that an object simultaneously has membership and nonmembership in the same class, it would be a simple contradiction. According to the rules of Aristotelian logic, the proposition would either be revised to eliminate the contradiction or discarded.

We can also discuss a class or a set from the next logical level. By making statements (propositions) about the classes instead of their elements, we can talk about the class of ideas, and then ask if our class of books has membership in it. Again, our constructed logical universe divides into two groups. A class of ideas is an idea, so it can have self-membership. No paradox occurs here. Once again, if we consider the class for membership in itself, i.e., self-reference, no paradox arises.

At the third level of abstraction, a class of classes, however, things go a little haywire. If we say that S represents the class of all classes which have self-membership, the question now arises: How do we categorize S? Does S belong to itself? Yes, it does have self-membership. No paradox has appeared; no rules of logic are violated by allowing self-referential statements, i.e., the class referring to itself.

We must now ask the same questions about the other half of this logical universe — NS, the class of all classes that do not have self-membership. This is where Russell discovered his paradox. If NS *does not* have self-membership then it belongs to "the class of classes that DO NOT have self-membership." But this means it *is a member of classes that do* have self-membership.

Let us return to our story. Russell wrote Frege a short note, which, in essence, said, "Dear Mr. Frege, I discovered a paradox in your set theoretical approach. Contemplate for a moment the set of all sets which do not contain themselves as an element." Frege received the letter when his second volume was going to press. Frege had a terrible predicament. At age 82, he could not redo his life's work. After considerable thought, he came up with a marvelous solution.

He published his second volume as planned and included Mr. Russell's letter. Writes Guillen, "In a rather sad postscript to his second volume, Frege wrote: 'A scientist can hardly meet with anything more undesirable than to have the foundation give way just as the work is finished. In this position I was put by a letter from Mr. Bertrand Russell as the work was nearly through press.' "[13] Frege solved his problem by suggesting that the next generation of logicians would have to solve the problem of paradox.

Not surprisingly, Russell decided to solve Frege's problem. His autobiography contains an fascinating account of the process. Russell writes:

> At first I supposed that I should be able to overcome the contradiction quite easily and that probably there was some trivial error in the reasoning. Gradually, however, it became clear that this was not the case. Burali-Forti had already discovered a similar contradiction, and it turned out on logical analysis that there was an affinity with the ancient Greek contradiction about Epimenidies the Cretan who said that all Cretans were liars. It seemed unworthy of a grown man

to spend his time on such trivialities, but what was
I to do? There was something wrong since such contradictions were unavoidable on ordinary premises.
Trivial or not, the matter was a challenge. Throughout the latter half of 1901 I supposed the solution would
be easy, but by the end of that time I concluded that
it was a big job.

During the years 1903 and 1904, Russell lived in the country.
Each morning he went to his desk and sat in front of a blank sheet
of paper writing nothing until lunch. After lunch, he repeated
the process throughout the summer of 1903 and 1904. He knew
that he, one of the cleverest people in England, was unable to
solve one of the most ridiculous problems in logic. Russell refused
to give up.[14]

Around 1905, Russell thought he had a solution to his problem,
"The Theory of Logical Types." Essentially, he concluded: "The
solution to the paradox is simple — I WON'T ALLOW IT. I
FORBID IT. A set cannot be considered as one of its own elements!" Thus, in a logical discourse, self-referential statements
are forbidden. In short, "Whatever involves all of a collection
must not be one of the collection."

The Theory of Logical Types was designed to prevent paradoxical mischief. As Watzlawick, Fisch, and Weakland explain,
"It should be immediately obvious that mankind is a class of in-
dividuals but is not itself an individual. Any attempt to deal with
the one in terms of the other is doomed to lead to nonsense and
confusion."[15] Logical typing supposedly handles these problems
by insisting that we always keep the levels at which we talk about
phenomena separate. If we want to use language to talk about
language we need to use a meta-language. *If* we want to talk
about meta-language, we need to use a meta-meta-language.

While, on the positive side, logical typing may avoid certain
kinds of linguistic nonsense and confusion, it creates problems
when we want to understand the observer. It supports the scientific canon of objectivity by separating the observer and his observations! The observer must not include himself in his observations. Therefore, he is forbidden to use self-referential statements.

If we apply Russell's solution to the "barber paradox," it would translate as follows: The barber should not ask if he can shave himself because the question is self-referential! It violates Russell's rule of mixing sets and elements. Von Foerster comments: "But, of course, ladies and gentlemen, these rules were made up by Mr. Bertrand Russell. It is his system of logic. And as you well know, self-reference is a common phenomenon. Just because Mr. Russell made these rules, must this mean that we can never allow a person to examine his or her own experience? Must the observed system and the observing system always be different? If we have two observing systems, i.e., two human beings, how do we decide who is 'meta' to whom?"

As Keeney aptly notes, if we always obeyed Russell's Theory of Types, our experiential world would be flat and stagnant. Bateson, Kestler, Fry, Wynne and others have demonstrated that humor, poetry, learning and creativity can only come into being when logical *mistyping* occurs, i.e., when the levels are mixed.[16]

Self-reference is a particular case of a more general notion, recursion. This notion is a central concept of the way von Foerster thinks about the observer. " . . . the organization of sensorimotor interactions and interactions found in central processes — cortical-cerebellar-spinal, cortico-thalmic-spinal, etc. — are of a circular nature. In other words, they are recursive." Recursion enters into these considerations whenever changes in a creature's sensations are accounted for by its movements, and its movements accounted for by its sensations." As we shall see in later chapters, von Foerster will use recursive computation, computation of computation, to develop an understanding of cognition.

CAUSALITY

Our favorite explanatory mechanism is causality. During the past 300 years, a time period marked by the ascendance of the classical science, western civilization has become obsessed with the exclusive use of efficient causality, i.e., a form of explanation where the cause *precedes* the effect. Although this is only one of several forms of causation available, its success in classical physics has contributed to our treating it as our only model for making explanations. When we are unable to make efficient causal explanations, we are frequently at a loss to explain the observed phenomena.

For example, writing about his experience with his teacher Don Juan, the anthropologist Carlos Castaneda[17] reports that he and Don Juan frequently took walks together, during which time Don Juan would point out things for Carlos to observe. "Look at this," or "Do you see that?", but Carlos could not see it. Exasperated, Don Juan asked, "But why don't you look?" Carlos said, "I do look but don't see it." Don Juan finally understood the problem. "Aha," he said, "Now I understand. You only see things you can explain. If you can't explain something, you can't see it. You are blind to those things you can't explain."

We unwittingly slip into a logical straightjacket when we allow efficient causality to run all of our explanatory schemata. A cure for this problem may be to understand the structure of causal explanations and the alternative modes of causal explanation that are available to us.

The triadic relationship of causality

We use causal explanation to explain the observation of change. We may observe objects changing their spatial position, chemical changes such as a liquid changing color or water changing into steam. We can also observe developmental changes such as the sappling developing into a tree or the child developing into a person.

A causal explanation contains three parts: a cause, an effect, and a rule of transformation, which may also be called a law of nature or a principle. The law or rule acts on the cause and produces the effect.

Consider this hypothetical example. Suppose I am holding a piece of chalk. I open my fingers and the chalk falls to the floor. A physicist watching me drop the chalk could say, "Here we have a excellent example of efficient causality, i.e., where the cause precedes the effect. I will identify the main elements in this triadic relationship. The effect — the chalk fell to the floor. The cause — Lynn Segal opened his fingers. The rule of transformation — gravity!"

Pop psychology provides another example of causality. A man's boss verbally abuses him, and to preserve his job the man says nothing even though he feels furious. We will call this incident "the cause." Our abused employee comes home and yells at his wife and children for no apparent reason. We will call this "the effect." How might this be explained? According to the psychotherapist, the man displaced the angry feelings he felt for his boss onto his wife, a much safer target. So, displacement of aggression is the *rule of transformation*.

Here are a few popular psychological buzz-words psychotherapists and laymen use as rules of transformation when making efficient causal explanations of human behavior: low self-esteem, poor self-concept, lack of confidence, an aggressive personality, fear of failure, or the old standby, the oedipal complex. Notice that they all suggest a one-way causality, i.e., efficient causality.

Aristotle and causality

Aristotle was among the first philosophers to contemplate causality. In his *Metaphysica*, volume VIII, he writes,

> "Cause" means 1) that from which, as imminent material, a thing comes into being, e.g. the bronze is the cause of the statue and the silver of the saucer, and so are the classes which include these. 2) The form of pattern, i.e. the definition of the essence, and the classes which include this (e.g. the ratio 2 : 1 and numbers in general are causes of the octave), and the parts included in the definition. 3) That from which the change or the resting from change first begins; e.g. the adviser is a cause of action, and the father a cause of the child, and in general the maker a cause of the thing made and the change-producing of the changing. 4) The end, i.e. that for the sake of which a thing is; e.g. health is the cause of walking. For "why does one walk?" we say, "that one may be healthy"; and in speaking thus we think have the cause. The same is true of all the means that intervene before the end when something else has put the process in motion,

as e.g. thinning or purging or drugs or instruments intervene before health is reached; for all these are for the sake of the end, though they differ from one another in that some are instruments and others are actions.

These, then, are practically all the senses in which causes are spoken of, and as they are spoken of in several senses, it follows both that there are several causes of the same thing, and in no accidental sense (e.g. both the art of sculpture and the bronze are causes of the statue not in respect of anything else but the qua statue; not, however, in the same way, but the one as matter and the other as source of the movement), and that things can be causes of one another (e.g. exercise of good condition, and the latter of exercise; not, however, in the same way, but the one as end and the other as a source of movement). — Again, the same thing is the cause of contraries; for that which when present causes a particular thing, we sometimes charge, when absent, with the contrary, e.g. we impute the shipwreck to the absence of the steersman — whose presence and the privation — are causes as sources of movement.[18]

Classical science, with its emphasis on quantitative analysis, reduced Aristotle's rich notion of causality to the efficient cause. As Rapoport notes, "In Aristotelian terms, this amounts to 'ignoring the final causes which beckon from ahead' in favor of 'the efficient causes which push from behind.'"[19]

A closer look at final causality

Final cause occurs when the effect *precedes* the cause. Cyberneticists who study goal-directed behavior favor final causality.

You may be thinking, "What's that? How can the effect *precede* the cause?" Von Foerster explains, "Well, in order to be here at 9 a.m., I had to leave Pescadero at 7:20. The effect, leaving my home 7:20, was caused by my wanting to be here with you at 9:00. Thus, the effect preceded the cause."

Final cause has certain advantages. It eliminates calculating the trajectories necessary to bring about a desired effect. You don't have to get everything right the first time. You have repeated opportunities for error correction. Von Foerster demonstrates:

"I want to give Mary, the lady in the first row, my handkerchief. First, I will do so using efficient causality, i.e., I will *throw* the handkerchief to her. Therefore, I must calculate its thrust and course. Once I let it go, there is no feedback, no capacity for error correction. (He throws the handkerchief.) There, she caught it. Excellent. But keep in mind that once it left my hand, I could do nothing but hope that my calculations were correct.

"But there's another explanatory device called final causality that I can use *to assure* that my handkerchief reaches her. (He leaves the stage by the side stairs and makes his way down the aisle, carrying the handkerchief.) See, I don't have to calculate the trajectory. I can take many routes to walk to her seat and hand Mary my handkerchief. (Standing in front of Mary's seat, he hands her his handkerchief.) Since my behavior is goal-directed, I could take many different routes. If I ran into a problem, I could simply adapt to it."

Imagine what it would mean if commercial airlines used efficient causality to fly us to our destinations. They would have to aim the plane, calculate the thrust, and launch it like a primitive rocket. The chances of reaching our destination would indeed be slight. Final causality practically eliminates the problem, allowing us to reach our destination within minutes of predicted arrival time.

Von Foerster comments: "Whenever you use the word 'because,' you are speaking the language of efficient causality. Whenever you use the words 'in order to,' you are speaking the language of final causality. You may want to try replacing the word 'because' with the words 'in order to.' Or, simply observe under what conditions you use each of these terms.

"You might say, for instance, 'I'm sorry I have to go.' The other person asks, 'Why do you have to go?' 'Because I want to . . . Hmmm . . . in order to meet Joe, I have to go now.' This is a statement using final cause. You are going now (effect) because you have to meet Joe (cause) in the future."

Circular causality

In the last 40 years, final causality has again become respectable in scientific circles. The reason is the emergence of cybernetics, the science of information and control. Taking a more comprehensive view, cybernetics uses both efficient and final cause, combining in the concept of feedback.

If we have four events — a,b,c,d — the traditional causal arguments took two forms: efficient causality in which a causes b which causes c which causes d; or final causality, in which d, working backwards, causes a. Cybernetics showed that when d feeds back to a, both causalities are operating, which cyberneticians call circular causality: a causes b causes c causes d causes a.

Cybernetics also addressed the age-old question: Is everything changing or is change just an illusion? Cybernetics offers a model of dynamic stability. Stabilities observed at one level result from systemic changes occurring at other levels. For example, the tightrope walker must constantly shift his weight (first order change) to stay on the rope (second order stability). The human body must constantly change to maintain chemical balances necessary for life to continue. Dynamic stability depends on circular causality.

Culture and causality

Von Foerster tells the following stories to illustrate how culture affects our understanding of causality: "Now, I would like to conclude my discussion of causality by suggesting that our culture plays an important role in our predilections for causal explanations. Many young people who joined the Peace Corps were taught this lesson.

"Several of my good friends worked as teachers among the Ibo, an extraordinarily intelligent tribe, who live on the west coast of Africa. They taught physics and mathematics, using experiments to demonstrate to the Ibo the *truths* of physics. When the Ibo students, who ranged in age from 11 to 14 or 15, watched the teachers perform experiments, they were dismayed. They said, 'Aha, these teachers do not know their stuff. They have to make experiments to prove it to themselves. If they really knew what they were saying, they would just tell us about physics.' In our culture the experiment is the hallmark of truth. Not so in theirs: it is authority."

He continues, "My wife and I had a similar experience when we had the pleasure of boarding Ignatius, a young agricultural student from Africa. You can imagine the culture shock he experienced living in Champaign, Illinois. He was terribly homesick that first September he lived with us. His main consolations were family photographs and a large black-and-white photo of his chief.

"Before the holidays, we thought he might enjoy getting a camera for Christmas. He was delighted. He bought film and began to take pictures. Within a few days, however, he came to me and complained, 'Heinz, I've just gotten the pictures back from the photo store, and they cheated me.' 'Cheated you? In what way?' I asked. 'You see, I used color film to take some pictures, including a picture of my chief. I took a picture of his picture. All the prints were fine except the chief's picture; it came back black and white! But, you see, I used color film. His picture should be in color. They cheated me.'

"I said, 'Ignatius, you're mistaken. You have not been cheated. The chief's picture will not have any colors except black and white. If you take a picture of a black and white photograph with color film, your picture must be black and white.' 'No,' he said. 'They cheated me! I used color film and the print came back in black and white.'

"I didn't know what to say. But at that moment, as luck would have it, my brilliant son, Tommy, a physics teacher, walked in. 'Tommy,' I said, 'Can you help us?' After I described the problem, Tommy said, 'Ah, this is easy, Ignatius' and began to explain the interaction of dyes and photons. When Tommy finished, Ignatius said, 'Yes, yes, very good. But, you see, I was cheated! I used color film and the picture came back black and white.' Please keep in mind that Ignatius was not an uneducated person. He was a matriculated university student.

"Fortunately, just at that moment another visitor arrived. It was my dear friend, John White, a Peace Corps volunteer who

had worked in Nigeria. 'John!' I said, 'Can you help us?' Ignatius
bought color film and took a photograph of a black and white
picture. He got back a black and white picture and now he thinks
he was cheated. Can you explain it to him?' John turned to Ignatius and in a loud, authoritarian voice said, 'IT DOESN'T
WORK!' Whereupon Ignatius said, 'Ahh! Now I understand!'"

CONSTRUCTING EXPLANATIONS

Gregory Bateson spent the last 30 years of his life studying
human communication, often describing how language blurs the
distinction between descriptions and explanations. Bateson occasion-
ally presented his ideas in a written form he called a metalogue —
a fictitious conversation between a father and his daughter.

Von Foerster is particularly fond of Bateson's metalogue entitled, "What is an Instinct?"[20] for two reasons. First, Bateson
points out that a law of nature is an invention. Second, he shows
that a hypothesis is a statement linking two sets of descriptions;
it does not link two sets of facts.

Von Foerster: "Here is a Batesonian metalogue which is particularly pertinent to today's discussion. He calls it 'What is an
instinct?' Bateson always begins his metalogues with his daughter
asking her father awkward questions."

Daughter (D): Daddy, what is an instinct?

[Von Foerster (VF): Now if my son or daughter asked me, "What
is an instinct?" I would, of course, proudly give a lexical definition, e.g., "An instinct, my dear, is the innate aspect of complex
behavior which is . . . " Bateson avoids this trap.]

Father (F): An instinct, my dear, is an explanatory
principle.

[VF: So, instead of addressing himself to the semantic significance
of her question, he immediately shifts the focus of their talk to
its *dialogical* significance. What is the political significance of
language? What happens when someone uses the *word* "instinct"

in a dialogue? What consequences does language have for our thinking and behavior?]

> D: But what does it explain?
> F:Anything, almost anything at all. Anything you want it to explain.

[VF: I hope you will see that something that explains everything explains nothing. Also, daughter suspects that. She says:]

> D: Don't be silly. This doesn't explain gravity.
> F: No, but this is because nobody wants it to explain gravity. If they did, it would explain it! We could simply say that the moon has an instinct whose strength varies inversely as the square of the distance . . .
> D: But that's nonsense, Daddy.
> F: Yes, surely, but it was *you* who mentioned instinct — not I.
> D: All right — but then, what does explain gravity?
> F: Nothing, my dear, because gravity is an explanatory principle.
> D: Oh — Do you mean that you cannot use one explanatory principle to explain another? Never?
> F: Hardly ever. That is what Newton meant when he said "Hypotheses non-fingo."
> D: And what does that mean, please?
> F: Well, you know what "hypotheses" are.
> D: Any statement linking together two descriptive statements is a hypothesis.
> F: If you *say* there was a full moon on February 1 and another on March 1, and then you link these two observations together in any way, the statement which links them is a hypothesis.

[VF: Notice, ladies and gentlemen. Bateson defines a hypothesis as a statement linking two "descriptive statements." A hypothesis does not link two *facts*. He indicates that we must investigate the descriptive domain, i.e., how we make descriptions.]

D: Yes. And now, what "non" means, I know. But what's "fingo"?

F: Well—fingo is the Latin word for "make." It forms a verbal noun, "fictio" from which we get the word "fiction."

D: Daddy, do you mean that Sir Isaac Newton thought that all hypotheses were just made up like stories?

F: Yes, precisely that.

D: Didn't he discover gravity with the apple?

F: No. He *invented* it.

D: Oh.

Constructivists, like Bateson, suggest that even something as seemingly inviolate as a "law of nature" can be questioned. Von Foerster says we should carefully observe the distinction between a *law* and a *law of nature*. One is a legal issue in a social context; the other is an explanatory principle. We mistakenly assume that both have the same logical structure. Usually the "law game" has three sets of players: the lawmakers, the police, and the people who must obey the law. If you break the law you go to jail. At least this is how the law is supposed to work. In science, we may say that planets obey Newton's "law of gravitation." But, what about the infamous case of the planet Mercury. Mercury disobeys Newton's law of gravitation. It moves around the sun not exactly as Newton would have prescribed it. Is Mercury punished? No. It's the lawmaker, Sir Isaac Newton, who is punished: His law is replaced by one proposed by Albert Einstein. So the "law" as used in science has a different function than the one we associate with our legal systems.

SUMMARY

In this chapter we have examined the relationships between language, thinking, and our view of reality. Language, operating below our level of everyday consciousness, structures our thinking by punctuating circular streams of interaction into one-way causalities. It nominalizes processes and unwittingly seduces us into habitual causal schemes for explaining the world. When paradoxes arise, shaking us loose from our traditional habits of logic and reason, we want to eliminate them. We long for certainty, holding on to the belief that the world can be understood in our true/false logic.

What if, as von Foerster suggests, self-reference is *modus operandi* of the human organism? Might we not entertain the notion of self-reference, even for a short period, to see where it might lead us? In the next chapter we will examine Dr. Humberto Maturana's scheme for uniting the observer with his observations by using subject-dependent language.

3

Maturana and the Observer

> Everything that is said is said by an observer to another observer who may be him or herself.
> — Humberto Maturana[1]

OBSERVER-BASED SCIENCE

Biologist Humberto Maturana argues that scientific explanations do not need "object language": "We can put objectivity in parenthesis." He advocates explicitly defining one's statements as subject-dependent, thus uniting the observer and his observations.

Scientists make scientific statements to explain observed phenomena. The process of making and validating these statements is the scientific method. Performed by observers, the scientific method entails four operations of distinction. When the operations are coherent, a community of observers declares a scientific explanation valid.[2] Scientific prediction, like all prediction, is not predicting what is going on in the objective world; rather, it is the prediction of our experience. We do not predict where the moon will be on a certain evening and time; we predict where we will experience the moon on a certain evening and time. Maturana has developed a method for talking about experiences.

Operations of distinction

Keeney notes that, "The most basic act of epistemology is to create a distinction. It is only by distinguishing one pattern from another that we are able to know our world. . . . Although this idea may seem intuitively obvious, it is only recently formalized G. Spencer-Brown's work, *Laws of Forms*, acknowledged as a major foundation for cybernetic thinking."[3]

Maturana notes that a significant part of scientific work is specifying the operations needed to make observations. He distinguishes four classes of operations that must be coherent to validate a scientific explanation.

1) *Make a distinction*: The observer specifies the operations of distinction necessary to observe the phenomenon the scientist wants to explain. In short, he writes a recipe specifying what actions an observer must perform to perceive the phenomenon.
2) *Construct a hypothesis*: The observer states an explanatory hypothesis. The hypothesis is a mechanical system, isomorphic to the system distinguished in step #1. The scientist hypothesizes that if his explanatory system is left to operate, it will generate the phenomenon he wishes to explain.
3) *Compute*: The observer then computes another phenomenon the system in step #2 will also generate if left to operate.
4) *Validate*: The observer then engages in operations to see if he can observe the phenomenon computed in operation #3. If the phenomenon can be observed, the explanation stated in step #2 has been validated. The experimental system is isomorphic to the phenomenon.

Maturana uses lightning as an example:

1) *Make a distinction*: On a rainy summer day in the midwest, under certain conditions, you will see lightning.
2) *Construct a hypothesis*: If clouds moved by the wind become statically charged through friction, a potential

difference will be established between the clouds or between the clouds and the earth. When this potential difference is big enough, a spark will jump between them.

3) *Compute*: If I put a conductor between the clouds and the earth, I can charge a condenser. If the condenser is charged, it should light a light bulb.

4) *Validate*: We fly a kite with a wire attached to a condenser. The condenser is attached to a lightbulb. If the bulb lights, the explanation is valid in a community of scientific observers.

Notice, says Maturana,[4] "the only thing you have to satisfy the conclusion (step #4) is a coherence of observations between #1 through #4. For this, observers must be coherent. You don't require objectivity. The scientific method (operations 1–4) permits you to claim that you have an explanation that may be valid in a community of observers. Objectivity does not appear in these operations.

"There is no way to bring in objectivity. You specify operations of observations that you must perform in order to observe. Scientific explanations are not subjective. They are observer-dependent — valid in a community of observers. If you claim objectivity, you get into trouble because there is no way of proving it.

"Trying to do so only leads to a muddle, a tremendous linguistic difficulty. We have a language that posits objects as if they were really out there, as if there were some way of proving their existence under circumstances where you can't. The whole domain of perception sits under a giant question mark.

"The problem," says Maturana, "is how to talk. I'm not saying there is no reality. I am saying that we cannot use the object as the criterion of validation for our scientific statements. We don't need it, and we don't use it! So let us not believe that, by claiming an explanation is scientific, we are saying anything more than we have an agreement in the domain of observers that satisfies these conditions (the above four operations) and that has to do with human experience."

Maturana defines an observer as a system with components and properties which allow the observer to perform those operations necessary to observe. So the domain of possible observations is determined by the properties of the observing system.

Unity

The observer distinguishes "unities." A unity is anything that an observer can distinguish. It may be conceptual or concrete. This book is a unity; an idea is a unity; an observer is a unity. We distinguish unities with language, and if we wish to have others distinguish our unities, we must specify the operations of distinction necessary to observe them.

It should be emphasized that Maturana explicitly defines reality as subject-dependent. Objects only exist for us as observers, and if we want to specify how others can have the similar experience, we must specify what "we did" in order to observe. Objectivity remains in parenthesis: (objectivity). Maturana is not denying reality; he simply refuses to use language that asserts that objects of perception exist independent of the observers.

As Spencer-Brown[5] advocates, "Our understanding of such a universe comes not from discovering its present appearance, but in remembering what we did to originally bring it about."

The following example may help to clarify Maturana's position. Normally, if you ask a scientist if unicorns exist, his first response will be to say no. His answer is predicated on objectivity. Only certain animals exist in reality. If you ask Maturana if unicorns exist, he will ask what operations of distinction are needed to observe one. If you reply that one needs to go to a museum and look at medieval tapestries, he will agree that under these conditions one can observe a unicorn. If one goes to the Bronx Zoo, one will not observe a unicorn. The point here is that he is not solipsistic. It is not simply a matter of making up operations of distinction. The scientist must specify the operations of distinction that satisfy a "community" of observers, i.e., his colleagues. But speaking this way makes it clear that the perceived object needs an observer to come into being.

Composite and simple unities

Unities are either simple or composite. A simple unity has no components. It is specified by its properties. When distinguishing a simple unity, the observer *cannot or chooses not to* make further distinctions that would specify the unity's components. The original idea of the atom represents our most fundamental *conception* of simple unity in nature, i.e., that which could not be decomposed into a composite unity having components. Now particles are conceived of as the ultimate simple unities of nature.

The observer can decompose a simple unity by distinguishing its components. When a friend bakes a cake and you eat a slice, two classes of comments are used to discuss it. Treating it as a simple unity, we say it is delicious, it is light, it is rich-tasting, etc. We treat it as a composite unity when we discuss the recipe. Using language, we decompose the cake into its components and discuss how they were assembled.

Composite unities have two characteristics not found in simple unities — organization and structure. A composite unity's organization refers to those "invariant" relations among its components that define and specify the unity, giving it a class identity. When we recognize an object and name it, we are recognizing its organization.

Structure refers to the "actual" components and the relations between the components which allow for the unity's organization to be conserved. A composite unity can have different structures while conserving its identity. An obvious example is the human being. Structural changes occur with growth and aging, but we recognize the unity as the same person. Every time we change our position in space, we change our structure but conserve our organization as a living system. Living systems are dynamic systems; their structures undergo constant change while their organization is conserved.

We are not just living systems; we are *persons*, a different composite unity, which means we conserve a different organization. During a lifetime we are many unities simultaneously. We may compose and decompose as a student, a friend, a patient, or any other unity. Each one is different, distinguished by operations of distinction necessary to observe it. For example, a rock star may not be distinguished by his drill sergeant as a rock star when he becomes a member of the armed forces. The sergeant sees him as a soldier and a living system. From the star's point of view, his identity as a famous person may remain intact. Thus, distinctions are always subject-dependent.

By shifting our use of language, we make explicit what the observer does to observe, thereby emphasizing that observation is always subject-dependent. Therefore, scientific arguments — or any arguments for that matter — cannot be validated on the assumption that objects exist independent of the observer.

SUMMARY

Maturana's system for using language avoids the trap of objectivity, i.e., of trying to find out if something is "*really* the case." Family therapists struggle with this question when applying systems theory to family dynamics. The question repeatedly arises: What is the "family system"? Is it primarily the marital dyad, the nuclear family, the extended family? Should the system be extended to include the community or nation? Maturana clearly specifies that it is always the observer who makes the distinctions. The unities he specifies come into existence through the observer's operations of distinction.

4

The Nervous System

The brain alone is not responsible for mind, even though it is a necessary organ for its manifestation. Indeed, an isolated brain is a piece of biological nonsense as meaningless as an isolated individual.

— Sir Julian Huxley[1]

The neuron: the aristocrat among structures of the body, with its giant arms stretched out like the tentacles of an octopus to the provinces on the frontier of the outside world, to watch for the constant ambushes of physical and chemical forces.

— Santiago Ramon Y Cajal[2]

During his lectures, von Foerster discusses the central nervous system from several perspectives, presented here in the following order: 1) anecdotal and historical material illustrating the perennial debate over the location of man's consciousness — in other words, which bodily organ is responsible for the higher mental functions; 2) the evolution of the "internuncial" which links our sensory and motor systems; 3) the structure and function of the neuron, the nervous system's basic component.

HISTORICAL PERSPECTIVE

For the last 2000 years, men have disagreed over which bodily organ produces consciousness and the higher mental functions. One group, the "cardiocentrists," located man's spirit or consciousness in his heart; another group, the *cephalocentrists*, located it in the brain. Until recently, the dominant view was cardiocentric.

Von Foerster comments: "Most of us celebrate cardiocentrist's day by giving loved ones heart-shaped boxes full of candy or greeting cards with hearts on them. Aristotle (384–322 B.C.) was a cardiocentrist. He taught that the heart was the seat of all mental activity. He noted that if you open the skull of either animals or man, and feel the brain, you will find it is cool. He thought this proved the brain was a device for cooling the blood. Without it, Aristotle said, the blood would overheat and begin to boil."

The cephalocentrists, first led by Alkmaeon, a priest and philosopher, insisted that the brain was the seat of our mental and emotional activity. Hippocrates (460?–370? B.C.), considered the father of medicine, and the Greek physician Galen (130–200 A.D.), appointed physician to the gladiators, both advocated the cephalocentrist position. Galen performed experiments which showed that pressure applied to an animal's brain rendered it paralyzed. But the prevailing thinking was Aristotelian.

In the 17th century, the physician Harvey (1578–1657), famous for his work on the cardiovascular system, assumed that the heart was the seat of our mental and emotional life. Harvey, believing, like his contemporaries, that the heart was the animator of the body, wrote, "The brain is deemed the prince of all parts. However, there is no disputing the heart because its sway is wider, for the heart is seen in those creatures that want a brain."[3]

The nervous system had been identified by the 16th century, but it was believed to be a conduit that connected the "animal spirits," responsible for the higher mental functions, to the material body. Von Foerster refers to this model as the "reticulist" view of the nervous system. The reticulists believed the nervous system was made up of interconnected tubes, distributed throughout the body, whose purpose was to carry the body's vital essence. One famous reticulist, the philosopher René Descartes (1959–1650), constructed the model shown in Figure 4.

Descartes wished to account for the behavior of a young man kneeling next to a fire. Von Foerster, "If the fire 'A' is near the foot 'B,' the particles of this fire, which move with great rapidity, have the power to move an area of skin on the young man's

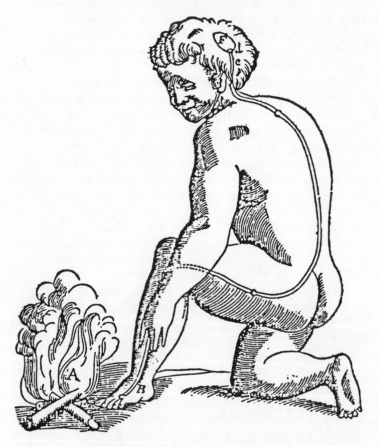

FIGURE 4. Descartes' Animal Spirits

foot. This, in turn, results in drawing the little thread 'C,' which goes to the brain. (This is just like pulling one end of a cord which is attached to a bell suspended in a church steeple, causing it to ring.) Now the entrance of the pore or little conduits 'DE' being thus opened . . . (now the important statement) the animal spirits of the cavity 'F' enter within and are carried by it partly into the muscles that serve to withdraw this foot from the fire, partly into those that serve to turn the eyes and head to look at it, and partly into those that serve to advance the hands and to bend the whole body to protect it."

Von Foerster translates Descartes' explanation into simpler language. "First, something pulls the cord and rings the bell. Then the door opens releasing the animal spirits. They, in turn, pull the foot back while turning the head toward the perturbation. This starts to resemble a description one might find in a modern behaviorist laboratory — only the behaviorists leave out references to animal spirits."

The first man to publicly advocate the neuronist position was Santiago Ramon y Cajal, a brilliant 19th century Spanish artist and neuroanatomist. As Knudtson describes,

> Born in 1852, amid the poverty of Petilla de Aragon, a tiled-roofed village in the Pyrenees of northern Spain. Cajal was the eldest son of a disciplinarian father who had left his farming to learn the surgical and bloodletting skills of a barber-surgeon and, later, physician. The boy had no interest in science; he was a truant and a mischief-maker occasionally in trouble with the local police for his pranks. His talent for art, on the other hand, was precocious, but his father could not bear his son's "sinful amusement." Finally Justo Ramon Casasus, his patience spent, dragged the boy, bearing a sketch of the apostle St. James, before the critical eye of an itinerant house painter. "What a daub!" sniffed the painter. "Neither is this an Apostle, nor has the figure proportions, nor are the draperies right — nor will the child ever be an artist." Triumphant, Cajal's father denied the boy all access to art supplies.

> He yearned for his son, as Cajal wrote in his auto-
> biography, to "renounce my madness over drawing
> and prepare myself to follow a medical career."[4]

Cajal finished medical school in about four years and upon graduation was drafted into the Spanish army and sent to Cuba. After a serious bout of malaria, he received a medical discharge and returned to the University of Zaragoza, where he received a doctorate in medicine.

It took him about seven years to obtain an academic appointment at the University of Valencia, where he began to realize his true calling, the study of neuroanatomy. In 1887, while in Madrid, visiting others "in the capitol who cultivated microscopic studies," he learned from Louis Simarro, a psychiatrist, about staining techniques using silver nitrate, developed by Italian neuroanatomist Camillo Golgi, a confirmed reticulist. Knudtson continues:

> Like other histologists, Cajal had found that conven-
> tional stains left axons and dendrites largely invisible,
> coloring only the cell's nucleus. Golgi soaked the tissue
> first in potassium dichromate and then in silver ni-
> trate, staining the entire length of neurons, whose ax-
> ons were unshielded by a fatty myelin sheath. More-
> over, it thinned the dense jungle of intertwined cells
> by mysteriously staining perhaps one out of a hundred
> neurons. But it could take days of soaking for a stain
> to penetrate. And perhaps because of the subtle dif-
> ferences between individual neurons, its performance,
> at least at first, was so erratic that Golgi finally aban-
> doned it. Cajal set out to refine Golgi's stain, and by
> 1888 he had already made a major breakthrough: us-
> ing bird and mammal cerebellum, he confirmed that
> nerve elements terminate in arrays that can be dis-
> tinguished from one another, and more important,
> that do not fuse with neighboring cells. He showed
> that certain nerve cells, for instance, send long, mean-
> dering axon fibers toward the dendrites of adjacent

neurons called Purkinje cells, wrapped them around them "like ivory or lianas to trunks of trees" but never uniting them.[5]

Unfortunately, what Cajal saw in his microscope could not be captured with a camera. The photographic arts were still too primitive. "To capture the details of a nerve fiber's undulating path through a thick tissue section, Cajal would have had to sandwich together multiple shots, because the lens could not keep the entire image in sharp focus throughout the entire section. By mentally creating a single, sharply focused neuron from many microscopic views, Cajal the artist communicated visions of neurons that no photographer could possibly equal."[6] The fruits of his artistic talents became the indispensable and necessary link in the success of his project.

In 1889, after unsuccessfully trying to spread the word of his discoveries with his own journal, *Triquarterly Journal of Normal and Pathological Histology*, he presented his work to the congress of the German Anatomical Society. There he was able to convert Rudolf von Kolliker, a well-known anatomist and confirmed reticulist, to what is now called the neuronist position: the nervous system is made up of separate neurons.

In the last years of the 19th century, Cajal's work was finally accepted. Using his slides and drawings, he conclusively showed that the nerves were not interconnected tubes but separate cells, separated by a small gap we call the synapse. Cajal's work marked the beginning of the end of the reticulist position. Completely reversing our thinking about neurophysiology, the discovery of neurons stimulated a total reinvestigation of the nervous system. Harvard neurobiologist David Hubel writes that Cajal's major publication, *Structure of the Nervous System in Man and Vertebrates*, published in Spanish in 1904, is "the most important single work in neurobiology."[7]

There are a couple of points that should be inferred from von Foerster's presentation: 1) Models of cognition reflect the prevailing scientific paradigm of their time; for example, Descartes' reticulist position supported his dualistic philosophy of mind and matter. 2) Cajal's discovery of the neuron forced scientists to reconceptualize their view of the nervous system.

THE EVOLUTION OF THE CENTRAL
NERVOUS SYSTEM

J. F. Fulton begins his comprehensive treatise on neurophysiology with a brief account of the nervous system's evolutionary development. "An appreciation of these early developmental stages leaves no doubt about the interaction between the sensory and motor systems and the nervous system's functioning as a computer that links detection with appropriate action."[8]

Elementary protozoa and primitive sponges are among the first animals that showed the capacity for motion. They have what is called an "independent motor unit." Their movement arises from little contractile elements. This organism is illustrated in Figure 5A. The round, onion-like object represents the muscle fibers. Protruding from the top is a small sensor shaped like a triangle.

If the pH value in the protozoa's environment is too acidic, the sensor sends a signal that results in muscle contraction; and if these contractors are universally distributed over the animal's surface, their contractions change the animal's shape. Thus, these contractions make a curvature in its body which, in turn, changes its sensations by changing the animal's physical relationship to

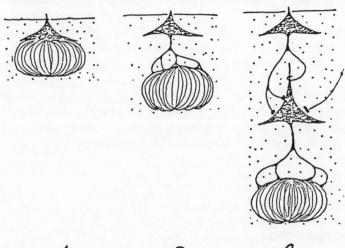

A   B   C

FIGURE 5. Evolution of the Nervous System

its environment. Its sensory and motor behaviors are interdependent.

In later evolutionary stages, the animal's motor and sensory units spatially separated. Figure 5B shows fibers that connect the animal's motor system and its sensory apparatus. This marks the beginning of a primitive nervous system. Equally important, at this stage in development, the elements of the system became specialized. Some cells were devoted to sensing, others to movement.

Figure 5C represents a significant advance in the evolution of the central nervous system. The connectors between the sensors and the animal's muscles are separated by other neural cells. These connector cells are called the *internuncial*: the "in-between" messenger.

Von Foerster refers to the internuncial as "the crucial step in the complex organization of the mammalian central nervous system. . . . It is, in essence, comprised of specialized sensory cells which only respond to a universal 'agent,' namely, the electrical activity of the afferent axons terminating in its vicinity. . . . Having once developed the genetic code for assembling an internuncial neuron, to add the genetic code 'repeat' is a small burden indeed. Hence, I believe that it is now easy to comprehend the rapid proliferation of these neurons along additional vertical layers with growing horizontal connections to form those complex interconnected structures we call 'brains.'"[9]

Thus, the evolutionary perspective presents a somewhat new picture of the nervous system, i.e., a set of sensors (specialized nerve cells) and motor units (muscles and skeleton) linked together by a network of universal sensing cells, internuncial neurons, some of which we call the brain. One usually associates sensory cells with the body's external sensors — eyes, ears, etc. The evolutionary perspective makes it clear that the entire nervous system is made up of sensors, and most of them are devoted to sensing impulses from other neuronal axons. We are most tuned in to our own system. The ratio of internal to external sensors is 100,000 to 1. That means for every rod or cone in the eye's retina, whose function is sensing external stimuli, i.e., photons, there are 100,000 neurons sensing internal stimuli.

Equally, if not more important, the linkage between these two systems shows that the sensory and motor systems are not independent. We do not perceive and act independently. This suggests that the nervous system functions as a closed system, a central point to be discussed further in Chapter 7.

The sensorimotor closure in the nervous system suggests the following propositions:

1) Movement $\rightarrow$ (change in sensation)

but not necessarily.

2) (change in sensation) $\rightarrow$ Movement

This closure can be used to account for mentation. Notes von Foerster, "Logical structures of description arise from the logical structure of movement: 'approach' and 'withdrawal' are the precursors for 'yes' and 'no.'"[10] Hence his aphorism — the logic of the description is the logic of the describer. Put in slightly different terms by Humberto Maturana, "The logic of the description is isomorphic to the logic of the operations of the describing system." We are the describing system.

This position is consonant with that of Piaget, who writes, ". . . the roots of logical thought are not to be found in language alone, even though language coordinations are important, but are to be found more generally in the coordination of actions . . ."[11] Piaget's notion of sensorimotor intelligence is linked to the sensorimotor closure in the nervous system.

Finally, in her book, *Philosophy in a New Key*, Susan Langer draws similar connections between movement, truth and mentation:

> The use of signs is the very first manifestation of mind. It arises as early in biological history as the famous "conditioned reflex," by which a concomitant of a stimulus takes over the stimulus-function. The concomitant becomes a sign of the condition to which the reaction is really appropriate. This is the real beginnings of mentality, for here is the birthplace of error, and herewith of truth.[12]

Von Foerster comments: "Truth arises from the notion of error, not the other way around. Only when you have error can you have truth. The truth must be the choice between appropriate and inappropriate action. If that is not there, the notion of truth does not exist." Thus, any logical device that always gives you certainty can never give you truth.

THE STRUCTURE OF THE NERVOUS SYSTEM

The basic unit of the nervous system is the neuron, the real hero of the central nervous system. Figure 6 shows a pyramidal neuron from a cat's cerebral cortex.

Cell body

The large, black blob in its center, which houses the cell's nucleus, is called the "perikaryon," i.e., cell body. *Karyon* is the Greek word for "pit" and *peri* is Greek for "around." So "perikaryon" means "around the pit." It is the thing around the nucleus of the cell body.

Dendrites

Shooting upwards from the cell body, extending in all directions like the branches of a tree, are the dendrites. They carry signals from other neurons to the cell body. Neurons can have multiple dendrites, making it possible for a single cell to receive signals from thousands of other nerve cells. This physical arrangement of many inputs to one output plays an important role in the computational capabilities of the neuron, as we will explore below.

Axon

The axon, a smooth looking structure when viewed with a microscope, carries signals away from the cell body to other neurons, glands, and muscles. A nerve cell can have many dendrites but essentially only one axon.

Propagation

The axon has a unique property of being an active propagator of an electrical impulse of about 80 millivolts. An axon is said to be *polarized* due to an unequal number of ions with respect

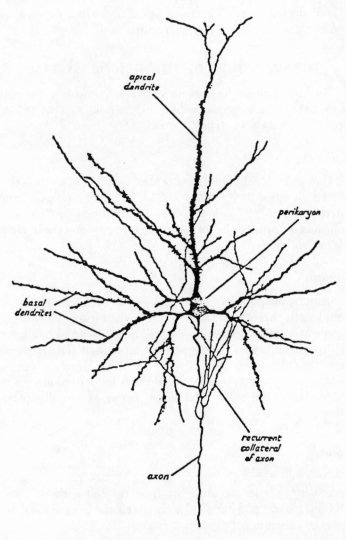

FIGURE 6. Cortical Neuron

to its inner and outer semipermeable cell membrane. This difference gives rise to the cell's "action potential" — its ability to generate a nerve pulse.

"The non-random distribution of ions leads to a *resting level* electrical potential of outside positivity with respect to the inside. To reduce the resting potential (as by some adequate stimulus) is to *depolarize*, a condition of excitability. To increase the resting potential is to *hyperpolarize*, or inhibit. If the axon is depolarized, there first occurs an *active local response* (i.e., short distance, nonpropagated). If the depolarization reaches a sufficient amount (*threshold*), a different type of response, a *nerve impulse* (spike action potential), is generated. This involves temporarily changing the permeability of the membrane such that sodium rushes in and potassium rushes out. The movements of these ions excite the adjacent areas of the axon to fire; accordingly, the nerve impulse can be said to be self-generative."[13]

Synapse

Neurons interact with one another at a gap between them called the synapse. Thus, a synapse is a functional connection between neurons. In Figure 7, one can see the axon (Ax) with its terminal button (EB) separated from the dendrite (D) at its spine (sp) by a minute gap (sg) called the "synaptic gap." The synapse allows the transmission of a signal, which runs along the axon to be transmitted to the next neuron via the dendrites. Compared with the axon's smooth surface, the dendrite's surface is rough due to the spines protruding from it, each spine linking it to an afferent axon.

Transmission of nerve impulse between neurons

The electrical pulse does not jump from one neuron to another. The synaptic connection between neurons is mediated chemically. A list of these chemicals, the neurotransmitters, would include such substances as norepinephrine, acetylcholine, dopamine, epinephrine, indoleamine, and serotonin. These substances have been shown to be involved in sleep, mood, and drive states, etc.

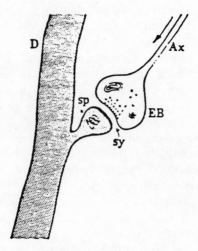

FIGURE 7. Neuronal Synapse

Inhibition and facilitation

Neurotransmitter "substances bring about a depolarization or hyperpolarization by, respectively, 'opening up' or 'closing' pores of the postsynaptic cell membrane. Each transmitter substance (there are probably dozens) is either excitatory or inhibitory at a given synapse, but not both. Thus, there are excitatory and inhibitory synapses . . ."[14]

Since a neuron receives inputs from other neurons via its dendrites, at any given moment it is receiving some combination of facilitative and inhibitory responses. As we understand it today, a complex function of the spatial distribution of these input values, inhibition and facilitation, results in the neuron's either firing or not firing, the "all or nothing" principle.

THE ENDOCRINE SYSTEM

Although not part of the nervous system proper, the endocrine system has significant effect on it and therefore this brief sketch is presented.

The endocrine system is comprised of several glands which secrete hormones into the blood stream. These include the pituitary, the thyroid, the parathyroids, the pancreas, and the adrenal glands. Depending on the specific hormone, a cell is said to be "inhibited" or "facilitated." Some hormones act on specific targets in the body; others act on all tissue. The endocrine system is associated with bodily homeostasis and the regulation of the body's growth and development.

The nervous and endocrine systems are interdependent. Each acts on the other. Of special interest for this presentation are the adrenal glands, which produce the hormones epinephrine and norepinephrine. In the brain, these substances function as neurotransmitters, playing a direct role in the postsynaptic neuron's action potential.

Thus, we have two interdependent physiological systems — the nervous system and the endocrine system — making a second closure in the nervous system. Activity in the nervous system affects the activity of the endocrine system, which, through its production of hormones or neurotransmitters, affects activity of the nervous system.

NERVOUS SYSTEM FUNCTIONING

Given these components, we may now ask: What functions does this system of axons and dendrites serve? We can get some answers to this question by examining an axon with a fine electric probe, a micro-pipette, an instrument small enough to enter an axon. Once it is inserted and its output is amplified and represented on a voltmeter and oscilloscope, one finds that there is an 80 millivolt difference (inside negative with respect to the outside) between its inner and outer membrane wall (see Figure 8).

"This is a fantastic system," says von Foerster. "If at any point its equilibrium is perturbed, the axon's polarities reverse. The inside becomes positive and the outside becomes negative. All the electrical charges in the immediate vicinity of the perturbation race to the location, attempting to compensate for this shift in polarity. This causes additional perturbations, which spread along the axon in a wave-like fashion."

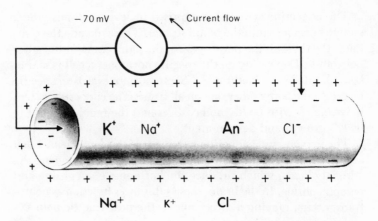

FIGURE 8. Neuronal Action Potential. The intracellular neuroplasm potential of the normal nerve fiber "at rest" is negative to the extracellular potential. Sodium (Na^+) and chloride (Cl^-) ions are high concentrations in the extracellular fluid; and the potassium (K^+) ions and protein (An^-) are in high concentrations in the neuroplasm. The potential across the plasma membrane is about -70 to -90 millivolts.

The following analogy shows how the nervous tissue propagates an electrical impulse. Imagine a theater full of people. Each person in the first row is holding hands with the person to his right and left. Suddenly, someone on the far right of the row lifts his hands above his head. (This is analogous to perturbing a sensor.) If everyone is to continue holding hands, this movement must be absorbed. So the person on his left allows his hands to be lifted and his neighbors do the same. The initial perturbation is passed from person to person, giving the appearance of a wave traveling from the right of the row to its left. Thus we have a signal. Each time the person on the right lifts his hands, we can see the signal traveling from right to left. This is what happens in the axon.

Encoding

Now we come to a key point in the description of how the central nervous system functions. Consider, for a moment, just one touch receptor. We apply some pressure to it and observe its response. If we apply only a small amount of pressure, we can observe a few pulses traveling along the axon, approximately five per second. If we apply a stronger pressure, the number of impulses will increase. The more pressure we apply, the greater the frequency of the pulses.

You can see how a chain of these pulses would look on an oscilloscope. Each spike represents one neuronal firing. If you were to put a micro-pipette into a touch receptor and amplify its output through an audio device, you would hear "p–p–p–p–p–p" or "prrrrrrrrrr," depending on how hard you press. The language of the neuron is electric pulses, whose frequency changes with the intensity of the perturbation.

We could now do the same thing to a different kind of sensor, such as a heat sensor. We would find, once again, that the frequency of the pulses traveling down the axon is a function of the strength of the perturbation. In this case, we would apply heat. Thus, we come to the central point of this discussion: *Electrical activity of the receptor cell, indeed, of all nerve cells, only encodes the magnitude of the perturbation, which is reflected in how often the cell fires. It does not encode the nature of the perturbing stimulus.* The strength of the nerve pulse is always the same. The action potential of the neuron, i.e., 80 millivolts, operates on the "all or nothing" principle. Either it fires or it does not fire. This is why the electrical properties of a neuron are characterized as switch-like or digital. But this is a misuse of language.

On the one hand, the frequency of the spikes coming off the axon is analogous to the pressure being applied to the sensor. On the other hand, the pulse itself is discrete; either it fires or it does not. However, "discrete" does not mean that the neuron is "digital." "Digital" and "discrete" are not synonomous concepts.

Digital has to do with the representation of numbers. Von Foerster says: "A digit is what is found in a slot. For instance, the roman numeral system is not digital; it spells out the numbers. Digital means that a number has a place value; numbers derive their value from a particular place. The decimal number 563 means 5 times one hundred, plus 6 times ten, plus 3 times one. This comes from counting on the fingers. So the nerve pulse is discrete, but the frequency of the pulse is an analogue to the par-

ticular perturbation. Thus, the argument as to whether the neuron is a digital device or an analogic device is erroneous. It is a
misuse of language."

SUMMARY

Let us summarize by considering the quote from Huxley that
opens this chapter: "The brain alone is not responsible for mind,
even though it is a necessary organ for its manifestation. Indeed,
an isolated brain is a piece of biological nonsense as meaningless
as an isolated individual."[15]

The last majority of neurons which comprise the central nervous system, including those in the brain, are universal sensors,
linking our sensory and motor apparatus into a closed system. On
close examination, we also find that the specialized sensors, the
rods and cones of the eye, the touch receptors, etc., like all
neurons, only encode how much stimulation they receive, not the
nature of the perturbing agent. Neurons, operating on the all or
nothing principle, either fire an 80 milivolt pulse or do not fire.
Thus, the nervous system, is an FM or frequency modulating system, encoding only how often neurons fires.

There is, indeed, nothing in one neuron or a collection of them
that accounts for the various mental functions usually called cognition. Only when we treat neurons and the body's motor system
as components of a closed, recursively functioning system, capable of computation, can we begin to account for cognition. Chapter 5, Computation, Chapter 6, Biocomputation, and Chapter
7, Closure, will address themselves to this explanation of cognition and its epistemological implications.

5

Computation

The term computation indicates any operation that transforms, modifies, re-arranges or orders observed physical entities, "objects," or their representations, "symbols."

— Heinz Von Foerster[1]

If we do not know that we do not know, then we think we know.

— R. D. Laing[2]

BRAINS AND COMPUTERS

One usually associates computation with computers. But computation has a much broader meaning. "Computation" has two latin roots: *com* which means "together," and *putare* which means "to contemplate." When you contemplate two or more entities together, you *compute* their relationship.

Naturally, one can compute with numbers. Depending on the operator used, one may compute with the numbers "2" and "3" in several ways. If the operator is multiplication, 2 *times* 3 equals six; if the operator is addition, 2 *plus* 3 equals five.

"Now," says von Foerster, "We must be careful. Computation takes place in the nervous system. Therefore, we can say the nervous system is a computer or computing system. But this is only correct if one understands the general notion of computation. If computation is not understood, we are immediately in danger of thinking the reverse is true — that anything which is a computer is a brain. Thus, the brain is a computer but computers are not brains or electrical brains. Furthermore, computers do not simulate brain functions as we do not yet know how the brain works."[3]

Many people associate the brain and computers. We may now ask an important question: Is there a relationship between the brain and the computer? Yes. Not all computers are brains, but all brains are computers; all brains perform computation. To-day's computer metaphors have misled students of the brain in-to believing that a functional isomorphism exists between computers and mental functions. Computers do not have problems; it is "we" who have problems. Computers do not process *information*. They process and store *data*. Anthropomorphizing machines has led to a great confusion between machines and what we do not understand — the brain. It has tempted many brain researchers into thinking that computers are brains and therefore the brain is built and works like a computer.

Someday computers may have memories. In the future this human capacity might be embodied into a machine, but this will depend on *our* first understanding what memory is and how it works. We do not understand memory, so how can we build it into a machine? This most important state of affairs may have been overlooked due to linguistic confusion.

Von Foerster says, "Since we live today in an era of science and technology rather than of emotion and sentimentality, the endearing epithets for our machines are not ones of character but of intellect. Although it is quite possible and perhaps even appropriate to talk about 'a proud IBM 360-50 system,' the 'valiant 1800,' or the 'sly PDP 8,' I have never observed anyone using this type of language. Instead, we romanticize what appear to be the machines' intellectual functions. We talk about their 'memories'; we say these machines store and retrieve 'information,' 'solve problems,' 'prove theorems,' etc. Apparently, one is dealing here with quite intelligent chaps. There are even some attempts to design an A.I.Q., an 'artificial intelligence quotient,' to carry over into this new field of 'artificial intelligence' with efficacy and authority these misconceptions about these machines faculties and capacities that are still today quite popular among some prominent behaviorists.

"However, in the last decade or so, something odd and distressing has developed. Namely, not only have the engineers who work with these systems gradually begun to believe that those mental functions whose names were first metaphorically applied to some machine operations are indeed residing in these machines, but some *biologists* — tempted by the absence of a comprehensive theory of mentation — have begun to believe that certain machine operations, which unfortunately carried the names of some mental processes, are indeed functional isomorphs of these operations. For example, in the search for the physiological basis of memory, they began to look for neural mechanisms that 'freeze' temporal configurations (magnetic tape, drums, or cores) or spatial configurations (holograms) of the electromagnetic field so that they may be inspected at a later time."[4]

Digital computers

Understanding how digital computers work might be useful to clarify the distinction between brains and computers. Computers were originally invented to take the drudgery out of calculation. In 1617, John Napier, the Scottish mathematician who invented logarithms, published his *Robdologia*, describing a method by which rods were used to perform multiplications and divisions. Known as "Napier's bones," these computing rods predated what we now call the slide rule.

Another precursor to high speed digital computers was built by the mathematician Blaise Pascal in 1642. Pascal's device used wheels and cogs to embody the decimal number system.

The decimal number system contains ten digits represented by the symbols: 1, 2, 3, 4, 5, 6, 7, 8, 9, 0. The base of this system is ten. The decimal system is a positional numeration system, meaning that the numbers get their value from their position. For example, the number 531 is equal to $(5 \times 10^2) + (3 \times 10^1) + (1 \times 10^0)$. Thus, we have $(5 \times 100) + (3 \times 10) + (1 \times 1)$, which equals 531.

Since Pascal's computer was based on the decimal system, its capacity to count or keep track of numbers (which is different from computing them) worked like a car's odometer. The odometer uses a set of interlocking wheels, each wheel containing 10 teeth. The car's rear axle drives the odometer wheel representing tenths of a mile. After one complete revolution, the wheel's tooth strikes a tooth on the mile wheel, causing it to turn one-tenth of a revolution. This is equivalent to a carry operation in addition.

The use of the binary number system marks the beginning of the modern digital computer. Unlike the decimal system, which uses ten digits, the binary number system has only two digits — 0 and 1. Besides purely mathematical operations, binary numbers can also handle graphs, letters, and processing instructions. The chart below shows letters and decimal numbers written in binary numbers.

Decimal	Binary	Letters and symbols	Binary representation
1	001	A	0100 0001
2	010	B	0100 0010
3	011	C	0100 0011
4	100	=	0011 1101
5	101	+	0010 1011

Binary numbers permitted engineers to replace cumbersome wheels and cogs with mechanical relays, i.e., simple on-off switches. When open, the relay represented a "0," when closed, a "1." Electrically controlled relays open and close faster than their mechanical predecessors, switching about 20 times per second. In other words, a computer using electromechanical relays could do about 20 calculations per second.

Around 1945 vacuum tubes replaced the electromagnetic relays. Though needing large amounts of power and therefore creating heat problems, vacuum tubes could open and close thousands of times per second, providing a substantial increase in the machine's computation power. Vacuum tubes (first-generation computers) gave way to faster, cooler running transistors (second-generation computers), which engineers soon combined into integrated circuits (third-generation computers), and then miniaturized, packing thousands of them on a tiny silicon chip (fourth-generation computers).

Since, in general, computers must carry out all their instructions *serially*, one after another, rather than in true parallel, speed becomes one of the correlates of computational power.

Super computers, like the Cray, can switch a billion times per second. The average home computer performs between two and six million times per second. But no matter how large or how fast the computer is, its fundamental component is a simple two-position switch that is either open or closed.

Besides performing the basic mathematical operations — addition, subtraction, multiplication and division — binary numbers are ideally suited for computing logical functions. In 1854, George Boole popularized an algebra that combined mathematics and logic. In 1938, Claude Shannon, working for Bell labs, found a practical application for Boole's algebra, the analytic telephone switching device. Following Shannon's lead, engineers embodied Boolean algebra into the circuits of electronic computers, enabling the machine to perform logical operations. Each Boolean variable is either true or false, which the computer represents as a binary 1 or a binary 0.

The formal study of these computations is called propositional calculus. Since we will be examining how the nervous system computes logical functions, we will digress briefly from our description of digital computers and describe how logical functions are computed.

Propositional calculus

Pospesel says, "Each day, each of us advances arguments and encounters arguments put forward by others. Arguments can be assessed in two ways. On the one hand, we may determine the truth or falsity of the premises occurring in the argument. This may be called assessing the argument's *content*. On the other hand, we may determine if the conclusion follows from its premises. When we evaluate an argument on this score we are assessing its form."[5] Assessing the form is the logician's task.

Logicians, following Aristotle's teaching, work with propositions (declarative statements) which are said to be either true or false. Since the logician is only concerned with the logical connections in an argument, he simplifies his work by replacing propositions with letters. Traditionally, logicians use the letters "P" or "Q" to stand for their propositions. The letter "P" can stand for anything: "I'm an elephant," "It is raining," or, "The moon is made of cheese."

Arguments are made on the basis of logical connectors we use to string together propositions. Although logical functions may seem foreign, we do use them continually in natural language. For example, "This package is sold by weight, not by volume. . . . If it does not appear full when opened, it is because the contents have settled during shipping." Or, "If the bank is still open today, and my account is not overdrawn, then I can pay you." Finally, a newspaper heading, "Curfew stays in effect indefinitely unless violence ends."[6] Consider the list below.

and	negation	or
but	not	or
however	is not	either . . . or
moreover	it is false	
although	not true	
yet	isn't	
even though		

Logical functions are computed. Von Foerster: "Now, to give you some sense of what orthodox logic is all about, I will show you how the logician *computes* logical functions using just one proposition I call 'P'. With one proposition only four logical functions can be computed: 1) affirmation, 2) negotiation, 3) tautology, and 4) contradiction. I will compute the logical functions, beginning with affirmation:

1) *Affirmation*

"I can affirm P; I can say 'P is the case.' Now, 'P is the case' will be true when P is true, and 'P is the case' will be false when P is false.

$$P : YES(P)$$

$$
\begin{array}{c}
T : T \\
F : F
\end{array}
$$

2) *Negation*

"I can also negate proposition P. You say $\overline{P}$, indicated with a bar on top of the letter. When P is true, $\overline{P}$ will be false. And when P is false, $\overline{P}$ will be true. If proposition P stands for it's raining, then $\overline{P}$ stands for it is not raining. Either it is raining or it isn't.

$$P : \overline{P}$$

$$
\begin{array}{c}
T : F \\
F : T
\end{array}
$$

Tautology

"Some propositions, called tautologies, are always *true*. For example, consider the proposition, 'The sun is shining.' According to Aristotle, this statement is either true or false. But expressed as a tautology it is always true, to wit, 'The sun is out or the sun is not out.' This proposition is true independent of whether or not the sun is shining. If the sun is out, the proposition is true. If it is gray and cloudy, the proposition is true.

$$P : P \text{ OR } \overline{P}$$

$$
\begin{array}{c}
T : T \\
F : T
\end{array}
$$

"Although tautology says nothing, but it must be kept in mind that this is on the purely logical level. On the interpersonal-dialogical level, if someone says to you, either in private or in front of other people, 'you are or are not a thief,' this may have an impact on your life. So we must distinguish the domains in which these things are said to make sense.

4) Contradiction

"Conversely, some propositions, called contradictions, are always false. We begin the example with proposition P: 'It is sunny.' Now the contradiction: 'It is sunny and it is not sunny.' This proposition is always false, independent of the sun's condition.

$$P : P \ \& \ \overline{P}$$

$$T : F$$
$$F : F$$

"Affirmation, negation, tautology and contradiction exhaust the logical functions that you can produce with a single proposition. However, we can also use two or more propositions. Traditionally, a second proposition is labeled 'Q.' So we have propositions P and Q.

"Two propositions can be combined 16 ways, generating 16 logical functions, as shown in Table 1.

"Let us consider the logical function 'and,' number 8 on the chart, written as P&Q. Propositions P and Q each have two truth values, true or false. That means there are four possible combinations of P, Q: TT; FT; TF; FF. This exhausts the list of possible combinations. We can now ask when the logical function 'and' is true or false. Logical and is true if and only if proposition P is true and proposition Q is true. Thus, from our exhaustive list of four possible combinations, only one combination computes a true 'and,' namely, if and only if both propositions, P and Q, are true.

"Examining the logical function 'or,' the chart (column 2) shows that three of the four combinations generate a true 'or.'

	pv̄p & qv̄q	2	3	4	5	6	7	8	9	p&q̄ v p̄&q	11	12	13	14	15	p&p̄ v q&q̄
pq	pvq	p+q	q	q→p	p	p=q	p&q	p̄vq̄	p̄&q	p̄	p̄&q	q̄	p&q̄	p̄&q̄	q&q̄	
TT	T	T	T	T	T	T	T	T	F	F	F	F	F	F	F	F
FT	T	T	T	T	F	F	F	F	T	T	T	T	F	F	F	F
TF	T	T	F	F	T	T	F	F	T	T	F	F	T	T	F	F
FF	T	F	T	F	T	F	T	F	T	F	T	F	T	F	T	F

TABLE 1. Computation of Logical Functions with Two Propositions

For example, we can examine the proposition: 'If either Bob or Joe attends the meeting, we will have a quorum.' If Bob attends there is a quorum. If Joe attends there will be a quorum, and if they both attend the meeting, there will also be a quorum. Three out of the four cases are true.

"Thus, logical functions are computational instructions. Logical functions generates a more complex propositions. This is clearly seen when working with two propositions, which allow for 16 ways of combining P and Q into a more complex structure."

Since we are dealing with a two-values logic system, namely true or false, computing logical functions can be embodied into a computer. Computer logic circuits, called "gates," receive two or more input signals and have one output signal. These gates permit programmers to write decision-making instructions.

A gate with two inputs can compute the 16 logical functions described above. The computer uses a binary 1 to represent true and binary 0 to represent false. Thus, the computer is instructed, if and only if both inputs P and Q are 1's, then output a 1. If either or both is a 0, output a 0.

The number of logical functions is *exponentially exponential* to the number of propositions. For example, when you have three propositions you can generate 256 logical functions, when you have four propositions, 65,536 logical functions. The formula is $(2)^{2^N}$. So with three propositions we have 2 to the (2 to the third power) = $2^8 = 256$.

As can be seen from Table 2, the number of logical functions increases extremely fast. Dealing with large numbers of propositions is extraordinarily complex. In Chapter 6 on Biocomputation, we will examine neural nets that average a thousand inputs

# of propositions		# of logical functions
1	=	4
2	=	16
3	=	256
4	=	65,536
5	=	4,294,967,304
6	=	18,446,744,073,709,551,616

TABLE 2. Exponential Growth of Logical Functions

and one output. If we consider each input from another neuron a proposition, the number of logical functions computed is astronomical.

Finally, we come to an extremely important question: What kind of truths do logicians prove? Von Foerster says, "Up until now, my presentation of the truth tables has been straightforward. But it fails to address a key question: 'Under which condition can I find out if a proposition is true or it is false?' This is a difficult problem, but there's an easy answer.

"Read the introduction to any book on logic and you will find it says, 'If you want to find out if a proposition is true or false, DON'T ASK A LOGICIAN.' Logicians only study what happens when propositions are combined — not if they are true or false."

Returning to the digital computer

Boole translated numerical operations into truth values. The computer can compare two values and determine if they are equal or if one is larger than the other. Each of these computations generates a truth value.

Programmers have used Boole's algebra to instruct the computer to make decisions. All conditionals, no matter how complexly strung together, eventually do the following operation: If _____, then do _____. In other words, if the conditional is true, then carry out instruction A; if it is false, carry out instruction B instead.

For instance: 1) A high school computer can be programmed to check student grades: "If a student has three or more grades below a C, send his parents a prewritten letter informing them of his performance." 2) A factory computer might be programmed as follows: "If it is Saturday and machine B is running, ring the alarm bell in the engineer's office." 3) A subprogram can be written which in effect tells the computer, "If the user types the word Q-U-I-T, turn off."

Let's examine this last example more closely, because it reveals what computers do poorly — understand natural language. The programmer has placed a code into the program which represents the letters Q-U-I-T. He or she has also put a loop in the program, so that every time you use the keyboard to enter data the computer will check the data and see if they match the code for Q-U-I-T. If they match, the machine shuts down. If they do not match, the machine performs some other instruction. The comparison is done by simple subtraction. If the answer is 0, it puts a binary 1 in a register to signify equality. It does not know what the letters Q-U-I-T symbolize.

Many people are dismayed by the limitations of computerized spelling checkers. The program checks spelling by matching the user's words with a list of words kept in a dictionary file. If a word does not match a word in the dictionary file, the computer lists the word as a possible error. It will *not* find fault with the sentence, "I live in a green mouse," when you intended to write, "I live in a green house."

Digital computers have taken the drudgery out of calculations and can do useful tasks. A computer greatly facilitated writing this book. However, as John K. Stevens describes in the April 1985 issue of *Byte* magazine,

> While today's digital hardware is extremely impressive, it is clear that the human retina's real-time performance goes unchallenged. Actually, to simulate 10 milliseconds (ms) of the complete processing of even a single nerve cell from the retina would require the solution of about 500 simultaneous non-linear differential equations 100 times and would take at least

several minutes of processing time on a Cray super-
computer. Keeping in mind that there are 10 million
or more such cells interacting with each other in complex ways, it would take a minimum of 100 years of
Cray time to simulate what takes place in the eye
many times every second.[7]

SEMANTIC COMPUTATION

As Von Foerster suggests, our comprehensive understanding
of logico-mathematical computations accounts for the successful
development of high speed digital computers. Von Foerster says:
"However, the structure of semantic relationships, embodied in
the functional and anatomical organization of our brains, which
makes us respond to and interact with others through language
and behavior, is only now being explored and slowly understood.
. . . I am still baffled by the mystery that when Jim, a friend of
Joe, hears the noises that are associated with reading aloud the
black marks ANN IS THE SISTER OF JOE — or sees these marks
— Jim knows Ann is Joe's sister and, *de facto*, Jim changes his
whole attitude toward the world, commensurate with his new
insight into the relational structure of elements in this world."[8]

We are continuously performing semantic computations, but
we rarely identify them as such. Von Foerster notes that "the
simple permutation of the three letters A,B,C, in which the last
letter now goes first — C,A,B, I shall call computation. Similarly,
the operation that obliterates the commas between the letters —
CAB; and likewise the semantic transformation that changes
CAB into TAXI, and so on."

Semantic computation helps us understand and solve problems. Von Foerster illustrates this notion with the help of a recre-
ational puzzle studied by Weston.[9] Weston analyzed the relational structure of semantic puzzles, particularly those known as the
Smith, Robinson and Jones variety. In these types of puzzles a
story is presented in the form of apparently disconnected statements followed by questions which appear impossible to answer
given the puzzle's original form. Consider the following example:

A train is operated by three men — Smith, Robinson, and Jones. They are engineer, fireman, and brakeman, but not necessarily respectively. On the train are three businessmen of the same names — Mr. Smith, Mr. Robinson and Mr. Jones. Consider the following facts about all concerned: 1) Mr. Robinson lives in Detroit. 2) The brakeman lives halfway between Chicago and Detroit. 3) Mr. Jones earns exactly $2,000 annually. 4) Smith beat the fireman at billiards. 5) The brakeman's nearest neighbor is one of the passengers who earns three times as much as the brakeman, who earns $1,000 a year. 6) The passenger whose name is the same as the brakeman's lives in Chicago.[10]

We are then asked to answer such questions as: Who is the engineer? Does the passenger with the same name as the fireman live to the east of Mr. Jones? In the problem's present form, these questions are impossible to answer without a large computer and a mathematical background. The relationships cannot be computed. By "recomputing" the data, however, the relationships can be represented, providing some chance for solving it. Consider the graph in Figure 9.

Studying the graph is much easier than studying the puzzle's original form, because all relationships can be seen simultaneously. Each line represents a group of facts. The first line represents the trainmen; the second line their jobs; the third line the passengers; the fourth line their locations; the fifth line represents salaries. Using elaborate algorithms, the Smith, Robinson and Jones problem can be solved.

LOGICAL MACHINES

When applied to human functioning, the concept of a machine has a tendency to put people off. It suggests something cold and inhuman, with little or no value in trying to understand people. Ross Ashby,[11] British psychiatrist and cybernetician, takes a different view. He suggests that one of the primary contribu-

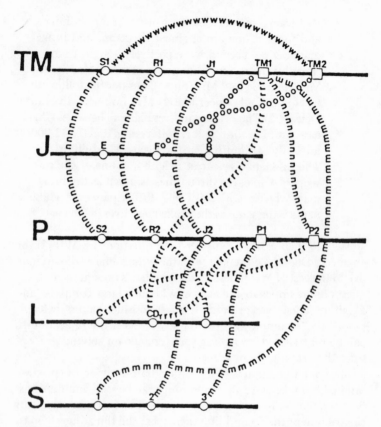

FIGURE 9. Semantic Structure "Smith, Robinson and Jones" Problem

tions of cybernetics is formulating concepts which apply to both physical and conceptual systems. He states, "It is, I think, one of the substantial advances of the last decade [the 1950s] that we have at last identified the essentials of the 'machine in general.'" Two factors had to be overcome before this advance could be made: 1) the idea that the machine had to be made of actual matter — " . . . examples can readily be given showing that what is essential is whether the system, of angles or ectoplasm, or whatever you please, behaves in a law-abiding and machine-like way"; and 2) the idea that one must take into account the concept of energy — " . . . any calculating machine shows that what matters is the regularity of the behavior — whether energy is gained, lost, or even created, is simply irrelevant."

Commenting on Ashby's article, "Principles of the Self-Organizing System," William Buckley[12] anticipates a second criticism to the machine concept, explaining, "Although such work may seem to some to be 'mere' abstract speculation, to many others it has provided a solid logical foundation for, and thus taken the mystery from, many of the emergent characteristics of the complex systems of special interest to the behavioral scientist."

Von Foerster uses the word "machine" to denote a conceptual device used to carry out computation. Contemplating things together must be carried out in something, and for simplicity's sake he calls that "something" a machine. These "logical machines" show potentialities and limitations of many concepts associated with cognition, including memory, learning, and holistic behavior.

Von Foerster sees two advantages to using logical machines as conceptual tools: 1) Machines "provide the most direct approach to linking a system's external variables, e.g., stimulus, response, input, output, cause, effect, to the system's internal states and operations. 2) The formal interpretation is left completely open and can be applied to the entire animal, or to cell assemblies within the animal, or to single cells and their operational modalities."[13]

TRIVIAL MACHINES

Von Foerster says: "I want to introduce you to some delightful machines that are really quite enjoyable if you take the time to play with them. First I would like you to meet what I call the trivial machine. He is a very reliable fellow. Whenever you operate him, he always behaves in a predictable manner. Most of the mechanical devices and gadgets in our lives are trivial machines. A lightswitch is a trivial machine. If you flip the switch up, the light will go on; if you flip it down the light will go off. Unless broken, it will work like this every time; it's 100% predictable. Let's examine this machine (Figure 10) and see what makes it tick."

A trivial machine has three parts: an input represented by the letter (X); a transfer function, represented by the letter (F); and an output, represented by the letter (Y). Consider a lightswitch. The input is flipping on. The transfer function is allowing the electricity to flow through the circuit. And the output is the bulb's filament getting hot and our seeing light.

We will examine a trivial machine with four allowable inputs and one output. Function Table 3 shows all the machine's allowable inputs and outputs.

Column X lists the machine's four legal inputs: alpha, beta, gamma, delta. Column Y lists its legal outputs, given a specific input. For example, give the machine an alpha and it outputs a 0. Give it a beta and it outputs a 1. If you give it a gamma it outputs a 0, and if you give it a delta it outputs a 1. This is a very simple machine. It is *completely determined* and *completely predictable*. (The input symbols are arbitrary. One could use the letters A,B,C, and D, and you would have the same machine.)

We can make this machine a little more human by attaching a voice simulator to it, so that every time it outputs a 1 the machine says "goodbye" and every time it outputs a 0 it says "hello." Now if you give it a beta it says "goodbye," if you give it a gamma it says "hello," if you give it delta it says "goodbye," and if you give it alpha again it says "hello." Giving it another delta gets you another "hello." The machine's behavior is perfectly understandable and perfectly predictable! No matter how

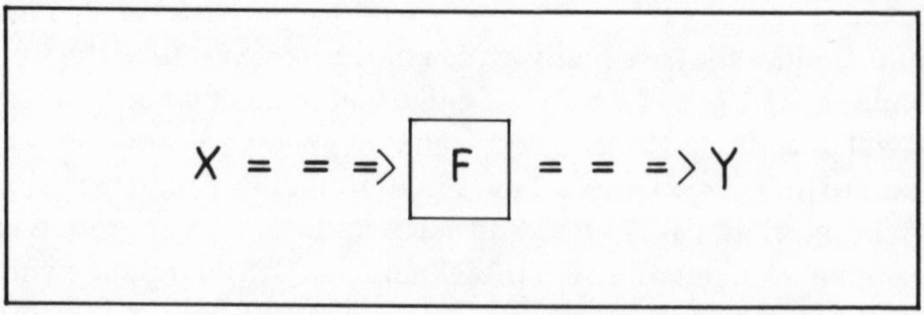

FIGURE 10. Trivial Machine

X : Y

---

alpha : 0
beta : 1
delta : 1
gamma : 0

TABLE 3. Trivial Machine Function

many times or in what order you give the machine its allowable inputs, it will predictably say either "hello" or "goodbye."

Trivial machines and logical devices

The trivial machine is a prototypical model of predictability and certainty. The trivial machine says, "Every time you give me the same input, I will give you the same output." Thus, trivial machines operate independently of history or experience.

This is exactly what we want causal explanation to do. Every time we have the same cause (the input), we want to have the same effect (the output). The causal rule of transformation which operates on the cause to produce the effect is analogous to the machine's transfer function.

Deductive syllogisms are trivial machines. The input is the syllogism's minor premise: Socrates is a man. Its transfer function is the syllogism's major premise: All men are mortal. Its output is the conclusion: Socrates is mortal. Von Foerster comments: "There is a machine called the 'All-Men-Are-Mortal Trivial Machine.' If you put in your friends, out come corpses."

He continues: "Suppose you ring a bell every time you feed your dog. Soon he salivates whenever you ring the bell, even without his dinner present. We can now apply the language of cause and effect to these events. The bell is the cause, the saliva the effect, and the dog the rule of transformation. I know that sounds a little funny. We usually think that conditioning accounts for the dog's salivating. But the dog is the rule of transformation.

"Of course, when working with living organisms, one must be extremely careful what is labeled cause and effect. For example, Pavlov, the famous Russian scientist, kept flawlessly accurate and detailed notes on his famous conditioned reflex experiments. Recently a Polish scientist attempted to duplicate Pavlov's work. Like Pavlov, he rang the bell when feeding the dog, and soon the dog began to salivate when he rang the bell without the food being present. However, during his final experiment, the scientist removed the bell's clapper and waved the silent bell in front of the dog: The dog salivated.

"So we must be careful about defining stimuli for living organisms. The ringing of the bell was a stimulus for Pavlov but not for the dog!"

NONTRIVIAL MACHINES

"Now, please follow me closely. We are about to enter the realm of the nontrivial machines. These are extremely tricky devices," says Von Foerster. "If obedience is the hallmark of the trivial machine, it seems that disobedience is the hallmark of the nontrivial machine. However, as we shall see, the nontrivial machine is obedient to a different voice. Perhaps one could say it is obedient to its inner voice."

Nontrivial machines have something called an *internal state*, represented in Figure 11 by the letter Z, which distinguishes it from the trivial machine. The nontrivial machine's internal state changes every time the machine computes an output. This machine is recursive; every time it operates it changes its rule of transformation.

The diagram becomes somewhat clearer if you look at the tables labeled A and B to the right of the machine's diagram. Tables A and B represent the machine's behavior in each of its two internal states. Columns X and Y represent the machine's allowable inputs and outputs. Next to the Y column is a third column labeled Z', which indicates the machine's internal state.

Assume this machine is also attached to a voice simulator that converts the machine's output (0 or 1) into "hello" or "goodbye."

The machine is in internal state A. We begin by giving it an

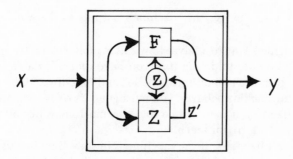

Driving Function: $y = F(x, z)$
State Function: $z' = Z(x, z)$

(i) *Read* the input symbol x.
(ii) *Compare* x with z, the internal state of the machine.
(iii) *Write* the appropriate output symbol y.
(iv) *Change* the internal state z to the new state z'.
(v) *Repeat* the above sequence with a new input state x'.

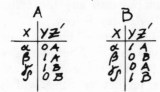

A		
x	y	z'
α	0	A
β	1	A
γ	0	B

B		
x	y	z'
α	1	A
β	0	A
γ	1	B

FIGURE 11. Nontrivial Machine

alpha, and it says "hello"(0). We must now examine the Z' column to see if its internal state changed. Z' tells the machine to remain in internal state A.

Next we give it a beta, and it says "goodbye"(1). The Z' column instructs the machine to remain in internal state A.

Now we give it a gamma, and it says "goodbye"(1). The Z' column shows that the machine changed its internal state. We must use table B to see how the machine will now behave.

We give it an alpha, and the machine says "goodbye"(1) and shifts back to internal state A. The change in the machine's in-

ternal state changes the machine's outputs to the *same* set of
inputs!

Imagine trying to analyze how this machine works by operating it. You are told only that you have four allowable inputs
which produce two outputs, "hello" and "goodbye." Observing
how the machine behaves, you must guess its rules of operation.
Most likely, you will assume that this machine is like all other
machines — a trivial machine.

After a few tries, if the machine is in state B and you give it
a gamma, it says "hello." You are tempted to think, "What
happened to you? A moment ago I gave you a gamma and you
said "goodbye."

"OK," you say, "I'll give you a beta." And you give it a beta
and it says, "hello." This is exactly how it responded a few
minutes ago. So you give it a gamma, and it says "goodbye." You
say, "Aha, I think I know how this machine works." So you try
a variety of inputs, hoping to discover a pattern or rule govern-
ing the machine's behavior. In no time at all you are completely
confused because the machine never does what you predict. It
constantly changes its internal state and, in a manner of speaking, operates with a different psychology.

The machine violates our "trivial" notions of causality. We
assume that a determined system must be predictable. Nontrivial
machines violate this belief. These machines have such complex
behavior that we *cannot* predict what they will do next, even
though the machine is totally determined and working properly.
Nontrivial machines are also unique because they operate in the
present. The machine's experience transforms it into a different
machine.

Nontrivial machines have an extremely complex behavioral
repertoire. Thus, the problem is to identify, i.e., infer, all the
possible machines given that we have a trivial machine with a
certain number of allowable inputs and outputs.

Table 4 lists the number of possible nontrivial machines with
exactly two output states. The machine we used had two two-
valued inputs. If we look at the last column in the second row,
we find the number 6×10^{16}. This meta-astronomical number
represents the number of possible machines our experimenter can

Let the number of inputs and outputs of a non-trivial machine be equal, and let there be n of them; then N gives the number of possible different machines

n	N
2	$2^{16} = 65536$
4	$2^{8192} = 10^{2466}$
8	$2^{3.2^{30}} = 10^{969685486}$

TABLE 4. Number of Possible Nontrivial Machines

potentially encounter when seeking to infer its rules of operation.

Von Foerster says: "Those familiar with astronomy or cosmology may remember that Eddington estimated the total number of elementary particles in the cosmos are 10^{72}. The numbers associated with the nontrivial machines are a thousand times larger than Eddington's estimate. That means that if you were to write each state function on a elementary particle of the universe, you would need a thousand universes. And we still have not discussed some of the larger machines noted in your chart. It is almost beyond our comprehension to grasp how fast the possibilities increase."

The first man who rigorously conceived of a nontrivial machine was a British mathematician named Alan Turing. During World War II he worked with the branch of the British Intelligence devoted to cracking Germany's military code. Turing discovered that the German code worked like a trivial machine. Although it was initially hard to crack, once he discovered its rule of transformation, he knew future decoding would be easy.

Determined to make the British code impenetrable, Turing developed a secret code which worked like a nontrivial machine. It continuously changed its rules of transformation, giving the Germans almost no chance of cracking it.

"It should come as no surprise that nontrivial machines are

very unpopular," says von Foerster. "Their unpredictability makes them extremely unpleasant. It can be a real horror to interact with something unpredictable. We love interacting with entities that are predictable. Our cars should start and stop properly and move in the direction we steer them. If our machines don't behave, if they fail to be predictable, we hate them.

"Behaviorists, particularly the Skinnerians, are experts at trivializing their laboratory animals, reducing them to highly predictable entities. Sometimes the animals become so trivialized that they die. This is a little too predictable, even for the Skinnerians."

Nontrivial machines tell us something about time. They operate in the here and now. We see this same notion of time turning up in the writings of Zen Buddhists and other eastern religions that question the notion of *one* internal, stable self. These religions argue that we have many different selves and that learning to experience these selves creates freshness and novelty in one's internal experience.

INTERNAL REPRESENTATIONS
AND THE HOMUNCULUS

Von Foerster comments: "While we're on this subject, let me address the notion of internal representations. These are all too familiar explanatory devices used to explain memory. You will repeatedly hear psychologists, neurologists and other brain researchers using these terms."

Von Foerster continues: "Concepts like memory, mapping, and engrams suggest that we make internal representations of our experience which we use to guide future behavior. According to theoreticians of this persuasion, I am now making representations of this music stand, the blackboard and all you charming people.

"To remember this scene tomorrow, I must reference these internal representations. Mapping is the same idea. Living organisms supposedly make maps of their environment and then use them to make their way about the world.

"Now, ladies and gentlemen, these charming theories are completely useless! If I make an internal representation of something such as the music stand, this means that in my brain there's a little music stand. At least there is a representation of the music stand. This means that there must be something or someone who can look at it and inform me of its presence when I use my memory.

"Now we come to a familiar theory — the notion of the homunculus. All theories of internal representation logically require something inside us that can look at the representations and inform us of their content. That something is usually called a homunculus. Homunculus means a 'little homo,' a little man, a tiny little man, who looks at things. So it is the homunculus who knows if there is a representation of a music stand in my head. It is the homunculus who gives me these data.

"But now an important question arises: How does this homunculus function? Does he have a memory? If the homunculus looks at that little music stand, then he must also have an internal representation of the music stand in his head. Does this mean that the homunculus has a tiny man in his head? Where does this stop? Soon we will be up to our eyeballs in homunculi. Besides, if we know how the homunculus functions, then we will know how *we* function. If we know that, we won't need the homunculus. We can eliminate him. There is a tool designed for just such a job called Ockham's Razor. It shaves off all unnecessary logical arguments. One clean pass of Ockham's Razor and we rid ourselves of the homunculus, the maps, and the internal representations.

"At the risk of confusing you, let me make a few additional points. The term 'memory' is useful in conversations or as a shorthand to refer to something else. For instance, I say, 'I don't remember' or 'I forget easily.' I'm *not*, however, using the word 'memory' or 'remember' to mean that I am unable *to access representations of a previous experience*. This is the key point I wish to make.

"We had the engram theory put forth by the Nobel laureate Sir John Eccles. Sir John spent most of his life looking for the engram — a localized function — and of course, he never found it. Near the end of his career he joked that he had begun to doubt if learning or memory existed. We also have the hologram theory of Stanford professor Karl Pribram. A hologram is a picture derived from a sophisticated photographic process. Lasers generate interference patterns which are recorded on a special photographic plate. Holography is quite fascinating, particularly its holistic properties, but the hologram will not help us understand memory. I would prefer a hole rather than a hologram in my head. Let me tell you why.

"If I had holograms in my head, I would be unable to think. Holograms can't think. They're just photographs. I would also need a homunculus to view them and an incredible amount of space to store them. You see, a hologram only gives you a single picture of what happens at the moment. For instance, standing here, in approximately a millisecond, I could make a hologram of what I'm seeing.

"Now, as you can see, I have taken a new position on the stage. So I need additional holograms. Soon my head would be so full of holograms that I wouldn't have room for anything else. Where would I put my homunculus? And even if I found a place to put him, in no time at all he would not be able to keep up with the volume. He would need his own IBM computer, and where would I put that? The holograms would take up all the room. Holograms do not help us understand observing systems."

TRIVIALIZING PEOPLE

Von Foerster continues: "We tend to trivialize everything, including people. Children start out like nontrivial machines; you never know what a child may do. You say, 'How much is two times two?' and he says, 'green.' 'No,' we tell him. 'You should say four.' We trivialize him. We invent schools and exams to test how well you have been trivialized. And if your trivialization is incomplete, you must repeat the class. A perfect score indicates perfect trivialization. Wouldn't it be preferable if schools would encourage variety in their tests?

"For instance, one might answer that Napoleon was born seven years before the Declaration of Independence was written. Must we always answer that he was born in 1769?"

The formal study of nontrivial machines, called the theory of finite state machines, is a holistic approach for studying systems.

The nontrivial machine becomes a new machine or system every time its internal state changes.

Von Foerster argues that human beings are nontrivial machines. We are recursive animals who change our internal states in response to our behavior. Thus, finite state machine studies support the view that we always function as a holistic system, in the *present*. "I can remember the past," says von Foerster, "but I have no direct access to it. The past is gone, ladies and gentlemen. I was standing in the front of the stage. But I am no longer there. No one is there; I am now at the back of the stage. I'm a different von Foerster from the one who was talking to you a few seconds ago. It's an entirely different Heinz von Foerster you see before you. The one that you saw a moment ago is gone. We all function like this. We act as a totality."

TRIVIAL VS. NONTRIVIAL MACHINES

Von Foerster: "The trivial machine is the mainstay, *the* paradigm, underlying our 'logical' working conditions in almost all fields of study."

The following is an incomplete list of explanatory schema which operate exactly like a trivial machine:

	Input	Transfer Function	Output
1.	Cause	Law of nature	Effect
2.	Stimulus	Central nervous system	Response
3.	Motivation	Character	Deeds
4.	Goal	System	Action
5.	Minor premise	Major premise	Conclusion
6.	Dependent argument	Independent argument	Function

Von Foerster continues: "These machines have the following properties:

1) They are predictable.
2) They are history independent. Whatever took place in the past will not influence the present.

3) They are synthetically deterministic. You can plug them together. You can synthesize them.
4) They are analytically deterministic. If you want to find out how they work, you give them the inputs, observe the outputs, and figure out the transfer function.

"By contrast, the nontrivial machine is:

1) Synthetically deterministic, i.e., you can glue a nontrivial machine together, just as you can do with a trivial machine. For instance, you write down a transfer table.
2) Unlike the trivial machine, however, it is *historically dependent*. What it does, its output, is determined by its experience, its history.
3) It is analytically *indeterminable*; you can't figure out what the machine is doing by operating it because it is too complex.
4) It is therefore analytically *unpredictable*.

"If one wants to use the word 'reality,' the nontrivial machine models the reality with which we are working. The trivial machine is just a hope, a predicted wish for the way we would like things to be. Maybe even more important, since most things are not trivial, we trivialize them. We trivialize complex systems so we can predict and explain them."

SUMMARY

To compute is to contemplate things together. We compute in many domains: the sensory domain, the mathematical-logical domain, and the semantic domain.

High speed digital computers can carry out millions of computations a second. Brains also carry out computations. Therefore we must be careful. We can say that all brains are computers, but we must avoid the temptation of saying that computers are brains. To date, computers do not have "memories" or "intelligence." Someday, these human capacities, symbolized by the above terms, might be embodied in computing machines. But if we are to reach this goal, we must first realize that we do not yet understand how our own memory or intelligence works. Furthermore, our ability to understand brain functioning is diminished if we mistakenly assume that the metaphors used to describe computing machine capacities, like the term "memory," tell us something about how the brain works. Brains do not have data banks.

Finally, trivial and nontrivial machines provide a useful conceptual tool for understanding the similarities in most of the explanatory schema we compute to explain our experience. The trivial machine epitomizes our quest for certainty.

6

Biocomputation

> Keeping in mind that there are ten million or more
> retinal cells interacting with each other in complex
> ways, it would take a minimum of 100 years of Cray
> (computer) time to simulate what takes place in your
> eye many times every second.
>
> John K. Stevens[1]

We are now ready to investigate computation in the nervous
system. As stated in Chapter 4, the internuncial marks the beginning of computation in the central nervous system. Comprised
of universal or unspecialized sensors, internuncial neurons receive
multiple inputs while emitting a single output, an 80 millivolt
pulse.

To compute is to compare two or more things together. Thus
when we compute, we make relationships. Computation takes
place on the neurological level. Each neuron, receiving impulses
from hundreds of thousands of neurons, performs a complex computation, i.e. computes a relationship, which results in the neuron
either firing or not firing. If it does fire, it passes its complex computation, in the form of an electrical pulse, on to the next neuron.
This pulse, along with those from other neurons, impacts on the
receiving neuron by either inhibiting or facilitating the receiving neuron's potential to fire.

Von Foerster comments: "If you look closely at this description you might draw the following conclusions. A facilitative pulse is like saying 'yes'; an inhibitory pulse is like saying 'no.' Now what does this resemble? If you are a logician, you might say, 'Aha! This system resembles the operations in the propositional calculus. Each presynaptic neuron is a proposition. If it emits a facilitative pulse, its truth value is "true." If it emits an inhibitory pulse, its truth value is "false." This system can compute logical functions.'"

NERVE NETS

Based on these notions, in the 1940s Warren S. McCulloch and Walter H. Pitts developed a formalism to explore the computational possibilities of interconnected neurons. Nerve nets were made of "formal neurons."

Figure 12 shows a formal neuron. The neuron proper is the triangular figure with a vertical extension pointing upward symbolizing the perikaryon (cell body). Each line with a loop around the top of the triangle represents an inhibitory synapse. The button-shaped objects located near the right and left sides of the triangle, called terminal buttons, symbolize facilitative synapses. Each neuron is also given a threshold value, symbolized by the Greek letter, theta — Θ.

A neuron's theta denotes how many facilitatory pulses are necessary to override its threshold and fire. If a neuron has a 0 threshold, one may assume it always fires. If its threshold is 1, i.e., a theta of 1, it needs at least one facilitative input to fire. If its theta equals 3, it needs three facilitative inputs for it to fire, etc.

McCulloch and Pitts[2] made the following assumptions about their formal neurons:

1) "The activity of the neuron is an 'all-or-none' process." [Either the neuron fires or it does not fire.]
2) "A certain fixed number of synapses must be excited within the period of latent addition in order to excite a neuron at any time. This number is independent of previous activity and position of the neuron."

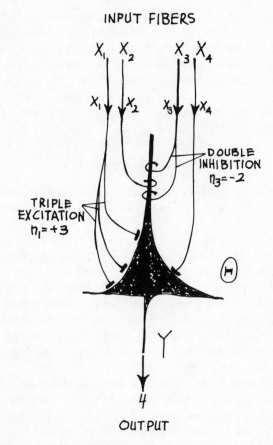

FIGURE 12. Symbolic Representation of a McCulloch Formal Neuron

[Von Foerster comments: "There are two points here. 1) Within a fixed period of time a certain number of afferent pulses must arrive to excite the neuron. Thus the pulses must come in *simultaneously* if the neuron is to fire." (A 'period of latent addition' is a time window in which simultaneous computation can take place, probably of some milliseconds in length.) "2) The McCulloch-Pitts formal neuron is a trivial machine. This system is not history-dependent. What happened in the past will have no effect on its operation in the present. This is a computing machine made up of trivial elements. They wanted to see what one could do with such a system."]

3) "The only significant delay within the nervous system is synaptic delay."

[Von Foerster: "You have to wait until something is coming about and this waiting is purely to be referred to as the synapse. The synapse will take some time until it transmits a pulse."]

4) "The activity of any inhibitory synapse absolutely prevents the neuron from firing at that time."

[Von Foerster: "One inhibitory input can prevent the neuron from firing."]

5) "The structure of the net does not change with time."

[Von Foerster: "The net structure does not change with experience."]

Now we can ask how inhibitory pulses affect the neuron's capacity to fire. The answer is simple: Inhibitory pulses are additive to the theta. Suppose a neuron has a theta of 1 and it has two inputs, one facilitative and one inhibitory. When the inhibitory input fires, it temporarily raises the neuron's theta to 2. If this neuron's facilitative and inhibitory input fire simultaneously and the neuron's theta is 1, the neuron *will not* fire.

Computation of logical functions

The simple element depicted in Figure 13 can compute logical functions. It shows a neuron with two facilitative fibers marked A and B. Depending upon the neuron's threshold, its theta (Θ), we can examine under what conditions it fires, thus what logical functions it computes. These possibilities are presented in the table accompanying Figure 13.

Columns A and B contain an exhaustive list of the four pos-

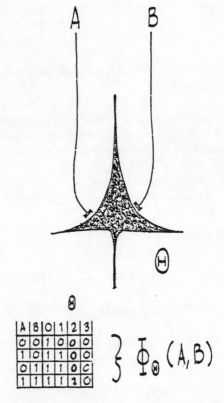

FIGURE 13. Computing Four Logical Functions with McCulloch Formal Neuron

sibilities of fibers A and B firing. Columns 0–3 represent four different threshold values for this neuron. For instance, we see under column 1, when the neuron has a theta of 0, the neuron always fires; when the theta is 1 it fires three out of the four times; a theta of 2 results in the neuron's firing only one out of four possible conditions, when both A and B fire simultaneously. Finally, when the theta is 3, the neuron is never firing.

We may now ask what logical functions this neuron is computing. To do this we only need to consider the 1's and 0's representing true and false. Under column 0, we find that, like the truth tables in the last chapter, all four possibilities are true. Thus, this neuron with a theta of 0 is computing a tautology. When the theta is 1, the neuron is computing a logical "or." When the theta is 2, this system computes a logical "and," and when the theta is 3, it computes a contradiction. It is always false.

It is also worth keeping in mind that the 0's and 1's are an arbitrary system of notation. We could just as easily represent true with a 0 and false with a 1. It makes no difference.

Table 5 shows, with two exceptions, all the logical functions with two input lines that can be computed by a single McCulloch formal neuron, if full use is made of the flexibility of this element by using various thresholds and synaptic junctions. For convenience, this table lists, in six different "languages," all the logical functions that can be computed with two propositions. The first column gives a digital representation of Wittgenstein's truth function (second column), taken as a binary digit number to be read downwards. The third column shows the corresponding element with its synaptic junctions and appropriate threshold value. The fourth column shows the symbolic logic; the fifth column the name of the logical function.[3]

Von Foerster comments: "The McCulloch and Pitts formalism is one way of *looking at* computation in the nervous system. Every formalism allows a person to look at the nervous system in his or her own way. Any time you look at it differently, you will get different computational machinery. It does not mean the nervous system is doing all these things. Rather, depending on the formalism you construct, you will be able to account for certain phenomena. Looking at it with a different formalism allows you to account for different phenomena. Unfortunately, this is a somewhat unpopular position, since everyone would like to have his or her formalism account for everything."

Computing invariants

When we view a moving object, its image on our retina changes, but the changes go unnoticed. We perceive the object as unchanging, as an "invariant." For instance, a wooden cube viewed

1	2	3	4	5
#	A B 0 0 0 1 1 0 1 1	NEURAL NET A. B. θ=THRESHOLD	SYMBOLIC LOGIC	NAME
0	0 0 0 0	θ=3	$(A \cdot \bar{A}) \lor (B \cdot \bar{B})$	CONTRADICTION (ALWAYS FALSE)
1	1 0 0 0	θ=0	$\bar{A} \cdot \bar{B}$	NEITHER A NOR B
2	0 1 0 0	θ=2	$A \cdot \bar{B}$	A ONLY
3	1 1 0 0	θ=-1	$\bar{B}$	NON B.
4	0 0 1 0	θ=2	$\bar{A} \cdot B$	B ONLY
5	1 0 1 0	θ=-1	$\bar{A}$	NON A
6	0 1 1 0	FIG. 12b	$(A \cdot \bar{B}) \lor (B \cdot \bar{A})$	EITHER A OR B (EXCLUSIVE OR)
7	1 1 1 0	θ=-1	$\bar{A} \lor \bar{B}$	NOT BOTH, A AND B.
8	0 0 0 1	θ=2	$A \cdot B$	A AND B.
9	1 0 0 1	FIG. 12a	$(A \cdot B) \lor (\bar{A} \cdot \bar{B})$ $A \rightleftarrows B$	A IS EQUIVALENT TO B
10	0 1 0 1	θ=1	A	A
11	1 1 0 1	θ=0	$B \rightarrow A$	B IMPLIES A
12	0 0 1 1	θ=1	B	B.
13	1 0 1 1	θ=0	$A \rightarrow B$	A IMPLIES B.
14	0 1 1 1	θ=1	$A \lor B$	A OR B (INCLUSIVE OR)
15	1 1 1 1	θ=0	$(A \lor \bar{A}) \cdot (B \lor \bar{B})$	TAUTOLOGY (ALWAYS TRUE)

TABLE 5. Computing 15 Logical Functions with McCulloch Formal Neuron

from different angles is still perceived as the same cube. Although its projections differ on the retina, we perceive it as unchanging. We call this invariance its "cubeness." Invariance results from a computation in the nervous system.

To illustrate form computation with a simple neural net, von Foerster says, consider "the two-layered periodic network, Figure 14. The upper layer represents receptor cells sensitive to, in this example, 'light.' Each receptor (top level neurons) is connected to three neurons in the lower (computing) layer. Two excitatory synapes (two of the four descending fibers) are connected to the neuron directly below. (This connection is symbolized by buttons located near the cell's body.) Each of the neuron's inhibitory

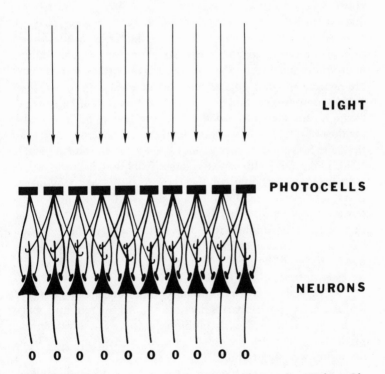

FIGURE 14. Two-Layered Periodic Neuronal Network — Without Obstruction

synapses (fibers) is attached to each of the two neurons below, one to the left and one to the right. (This connection is symbolized by the fiber circling the top of the cell body.)

"The computing layer (the bottom layer of cells) will not respond to uniform light projected on to the receptor layer (the top layer of cells) because the two excitatory stimuli on the computer neuron will be exactly compensated by the inhibitory signals coming from the two lateral receptors. This zero response will prevail under the strongest and weakest stimulation as well as to slow or rapid changes in illumination. The legitimate question may now arise: 'Why is this complex apparatus doing nothing?'

"Consider now Figure 15, in which an obstruction is placed in the light path illuminating the top layer (receptor) cells. Again, all the neurons of the lower layer remain silent, except for the ones at the edges of the obstruction, for they receive two excitatory signals from the receptor above, but *only one inhibitory signal* from the sensor to the left. It does not matter how many neurons are blocked by the bar; what is important is that there are neurons on each edge of the obstruction.

"We now understand the important function of this net; it computes any spatial *variation* in the visual field of this 'eye,' independent of intensity of the ambient light and its temporal variation, and independent of place and extension of the obstruction."[4]

Von Foerster: "This system is laterally inhibited. This is an extremely important notion running throughout the neurophysiology literature. People like Maturana and Eccles claim the entire nervous system is *nothing but* lateral inhibition. We have central facilitation-lateral inhibition. This system always sharpens our capacity to perceive change. This is the physiology that allows us to perceive 'difference' or 'change.' This system perceives a difference that makes a difference.

"Seeing change is of evolutionary importance. For example, a lizard sitting perfectly still does not see. All the rods and cones of the eye are flooded with inhibitory pulses. If nothing is moving in its visual field, the only way it can see is to move its head up and down very rapidly."

This net also counts the number of obstructions, independent of their size or position. Given 25 obstructions, the number of

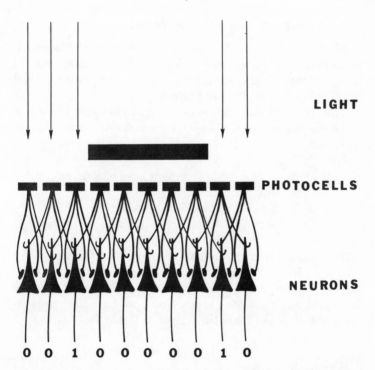

FIGURE 15. Two-Layered Periodic Neuronal Network — With Obstruction

entities in the visual field is 25. That means this system sees N-ness, where N is a variable whose value is the number of objects in the visual field.

This net *doesn't need time* to count. It is not performing addition. The firing of two bottom layer neurons is a different experience than the firing of four, six or eight neurons. The net computes the entire gestalt at once. It processes in parallel — all at once — rather than serially, i.e., one at a time.

Von Foerster comments: "I wanted to show you how nerve nets work because similar neural computations occur throughout the central nervous system. My drawing used nets in which each layer only had 11 neurons. A similar net in the nervous system would use many thousands of neurons."

What the frog's eye tells the frog's brain

About 20 years ago, Jerome Lettvin, Humberto Maturana, McCulloch, and Pitts completed a remarkable study of nerve nets, reporting their work in a fascinating paper called, "What the Frog's Eye Tells the Frog's Brain."[5]

They claimed that the frog's eye tells (computes) its brain about the presence of four properties, which can be stated in four questions:

1) Does the object of perception have a sharp edge?
2) Is the object round?
3) If the object is round, how round?
4) Do the edges of the object have a sharp curvature?

They argued that anything small, round and black may be a bug, something the frog may eat. So the net detects bugs. It also reports the presence of long shadows, like a bird's wing. So the net warns of immediate danger. Thus, we have the computational software built into the system as "biological hardware."

McCulloch and Pitts

Warren McCulloch, a philosopher and neurophysiologist, and Walter Pitts, a mathematician and neurophysiologist, made the first formal study of nerve nets in 1943. Their landmark study was published in a paper entitled, "A Logical Calculus of Ideas Immanent in Nervous Activity," in the *Bulletin of Mathematical Biophysics*.[6] McCulloch and Pitts showed that any behavior that could be described unambiguously and clearly, in a finite number of words, could be computed by a nerve net. For ever unambiguous description of behavior, they could design an appropriate nerve net.

Von Foerster says: "When their paper was first published, everyone interested in the brain and cognition said, 'We have it. We've got the answer. Now we understand what's going on in the nervous system. If you can describe a particular behavior, we can generate an appropriate nerve net to account for it.

Therefore, we can make the inverse conclusion: Since we have certain behavior, there must be corresponding nerve nets in the central nervous system that compute the behavior.'"

Commenting on the McCulloch-Pitts formalism in 1951, mathematician John Von Neumann stated, "It has often been claimed that the activities and functions of the human nervous system are so complicated that no ordinary mechanism could possibly perform them. . . . The McCulloch-Pitts result puts an end to this. It proves that anything can be completely and unambiguously put into words is *ipso facto* realizable by a suitable finite neural network."[7]

The problem of unambiguous descriptions

The McCulloch-Pitts formalism depends on "unambiguous" descriptions. Thus, the problem — there is no way to make "unambiguous statements."

Von Foerster comments: "Every statement, utterance or description is intrinsically ambiguous. Ambiguity arises when you fight with your friends, your loved ones, or your enemies. The difficulty is saying something that might be understood. We use the term 'misunderstanding' to explain our differences with other people. Ladies and gentlemen, let me suggest that this is rarely the case. If we misunderstood each other things would be a lot easier. No. We *think* that we 'really' understand each other. That's the problem!"

For instance, linguists often illustrate ambiguity with the sentence: "Time flies like an arrow." You can interpret this sentence 16 different ways, depending on whether you treat the word "time" as a noun or a verb. Time goes by. You can time something. Time flies. The reader may wish to find further examples.

Von Foerster notes, "Ambiguity is also manifest when you translate a sentence into another language and then retranslate it back into the original language." Translate the English proverb, "Out of sight, out of mind," into Chinese, and then translate the Chinese translation back into English, you end up with "Blind moron."

Admittedly, ambiguity flaws the McCulloch-Pitts theorem.

But the flaw has a simple solution. Ignore it! McCulloch and Pitts showed that they could design a nerve net that would generate (compute) any unambiguous behavior. Thus, we have a matching of two formalisms — the net and language. Obviously, language is ambiguous. Our purpose, however, is to understand how the nervous system works, not to match two formalisms.

Two more points of interest

1) Von Foerster: "Let's consider the ratio between our internal and external sensors. We have about 100 or 200 million external sensors. This would include the sensors in eyes, ears, nose, mouth, and surface of the skin. These sensors receive external perturbations. Our brain has 10^{10} neurons, i.e., internal sensors, which sense electrical impulses from other neurons. This means we are *one hundred thousand times more sensitive to ourselves than to the so-called outside world.*"

2) Chapter 5 described the exponentially-exponential relationship between the number of propositions and number of logical functions they can compute. Two propositions can compute 16 functions; three propositions can compute 256, etc. Each neuron's dendritic spine makes a synaptic connection with another neuron. The average neuron has between 1,000 to 10,000 synaptic connections. A single Purkinje cell (neuron) has about one million synapes. It handles roughly a million propositions.

SUMMARY

First, the firing of each neuron depends on multiple inputs from other neurons. Thus, the firing of each neuron is a computation!

Second, the input each neuron receives is a computation, as I will show in a moment. Thus, the nervous system computes its own computations.

We usually think the transmission of the nerve impulse is analogous to electrical current traveling a broken wire. When reaching the gap, analogous to the synapse in nervous tissue, the current jumps across and continues its journey. In the nervous system the gap is bridged chemically. This description is analogous to a relay race. Each runner passes the baton to the next runner — the same baton! *This conceptualization is wrong.*

The nervous system does not work like this. Although each axonal pulse has the same amplitude, roughly 80 millivolts, each pulse is the product of a computation involving thousands of neurons working in concert. The system transmits computations. The output of neuron A, a complex computation, becomes one of many imputs involved in the computation that results in the firing or non-firing of neuron B. Thus, this system computes its own computations, a completely different notion than a simple relay.

Third, the notion of the nerve nets described in this chapter offers a potent model which can be used to account for the richness of human experience. If we treat neurons as binary elements having two values, we can calculate the possible number of different nets that can be formed with a finite number of neurons. This formula is 2 to the Nth (number of elements) squared. A three-element net would have 2^9 or 512 possible nets. A four-element net allows for the formation of 65,536 possible combinations or nets! Ten neurons can generate 10^{100} number of possible nets. As stated above, a Purkinje neuron has about one million inputs. It can form 2 to the $1,000,000^2$ nets!

Fourth, to simplify the presentation, the biocomputations described in this chapter have been presented as linear processes. The linear view — input$\rightarrow$computation$\rightarrow$output — fits the more general assumption that the nervous system is an open system, i.e., that our sensory and motor systems operate independently. But as evolutionary studies of the nervous system indicate, there is a closure between our sensory and motor systems. Perception and action are interdependent. (See Chapter 5.)

We are now ready to discuss one of the most difficult concepts in von Foerster's and Maturana's models — a closed nervous system. What does it mean when they say the nervous system has no inputs or outputs; it has only perturbations? Unlike the body, which is thermodynamically open, literally taking energy in, the nervous system, they claim, is closed! So we are ready to examine computation of computation, in a closed system.

7

Closure

> On the one hand, our cognition is in our biological substrate as body; on the other hand, our descriptions are fully capable of self-descriptions at indefinitely many levels. Through the nervous system, these two modes of closure are superimposed so as to constitute that closest and most elusive of all experiences: ourselves.
>
> — Francisco Varela[1]

CLOSURE IN DIFFERENT FIELDS

Closure appears in many different fields, including thermodynamics, mathematics, biology, and general systems theory.

Thermodynamic closure

Energy can not enter or exit a thermodynamically closed system. Closed systems have an "adiabatic" surface that prohibits the passage of heat, energy and radiation. Living organisms are thermodynamically open; energy, measured in calories (units of energy), enters the body as food and exits as waste products.

Algebraic closure

In an closed algebraic system, each and every operation must produce elements which belong to the system's set of elements.

Let the system's elements be the natural numbers (positive, whole numbers) and consider addition. Adding 5 and 6 produces 11, a natural number. Multiplying two numbers also generates natural numbers. Thus, if you have an algebraic system in which a) the elements are natural numbers and b) the operations are addition and multiplication, the system is said to be "algebraically closed."

However, if you subtract 5 from 3, a problem arises, because this operation generates a negative number. Hence, under subtraction the system is no longer closed. To subtract 5 from 3 and maintain the system's closure, we must invent new numbers, thus creating new boundary conditions within system. If negative numbers become part of the element set, then subtraction can be performed and the system will still be algebraically closed. Adding negative numbers expands the boundary conditions, enriching the system.

Division creates new problems. If the system is to remain closed, the system's elements must be expanded to include fractions. Historically, this is how new numbers were invented. As the need arose for new mathematical operations, new numbers were invented which maintained the system's closure.

As Watzlawick explains, "For the Greek mathematicians, numbers were concrete, real, perceivable magnitudes understood as the properties of equally real objects. Thus geometry was concerned with measuring and arithmetic with counting. Oswald Spengler, in his lucid chapter 'On the Meaning of Numbers,' shows not only how the notion of zero as a number was unthinkable, but also that the negative magnitudes had no place in the reality of the classical world. . . . The idea that numbers were the expression of magnitudes remained dominant for two thousand years. . . . "[2]

Systemic closure

Von Foerster: "I would now like to present the notion of systemic closure. First, I will describe it. Second, I will discuss it from a conceptual perspective. Third, I will comment on the philosophical implications of closed systems, the notions of autonomy and responsibility. Fourth, in an oversimplified and compressed fashion, I will present 'recursive function theory,' a formalism we can use to handle the notion of systemic closure. A formalism provides a mathematical representation that allows us to illustrate and manipulate conceptual ideas. This can be extremely advantageous."

An entity is systemically closed when its elements generate each other by production operations in the system. Let me illustrate this concept by describing an "autocatalytic breeder," a simply but reasonably sophisticated closed system.

An autocatalytic breeder (Figure 16) works in the following manner: Suppose the system contains two chemical elements, A and B. Chemically, they do not react with each other. This may be a problem because you want them to join and form compound AB. They can be tricked into joining by introducing the catalyst

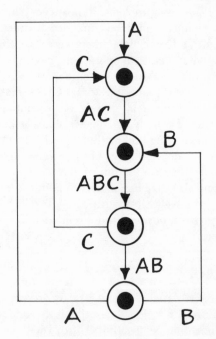

FIGURE 16. Autocatalytic Breeder

C, which will combine with A, forming AC. AC will in turn re-act with B, forming another new compound ABC. Then the cat-alyst separates from element ABC, as if to say, "I've done my job, I'm leaving," and AB remains. This is autocatalysis.

Essentially, this is what occurs in many pharmaceutical labo-ratories. Compound AB is produced with an autocatalytic breed-er. Oversimplified, drug companies feed the machine A's, B's, and C's and syphon off the compound AB.

Von Foerster comments: "This system is chemically and sys-temically closed. The elements participate in their own produc-tion. Do living organisms have the same processes going on in their bodies? A group of Chilean philosophers, familiar with autocat-alytic breeders, say yes. 'If we look at the organization of a liv-ing system,' they say, 'we see components — the DNA's, the pep-tides, the peptide chains, etc. — whose interaction produces them-selves.' These processes are not random or undefined. They're called *autopoiesis*, the system which composes, creates, invents itself."

AUTOPOIESIS

The term "autopoiesis" was coined by three Chilean neuro-philosophers, Varela, Maturana, and Uribe. Autopoiesis comes from two Greek words: *auto* (self), and *poiesis* (poetry or a mak-ing). It suggests something that makes itself. Chapter 3 described Maturana's definition of a unity as something with structure and organization. Organization gives the unity its class identity; struc-ture can change as long as the organization is conserved. Matur-ana defines autopoiesis as the "organization" of living systems. Thus, autopoiesis identifies specific interactive processes between components which produce the substrate consisting of these com-ponents.

Andrew defines autopoiesis as "the capacity that living systems have to develop and maintain their own organization, the organ-ization which is developed and maintained being identical with that which performs the development and maintenance."[3] Varela describes an autopoietic machine as "a homeostatic (or, rather, a relations-static) system that has its own organization (defining network of relations) as a fundamental varient."[4] As Keeney explains, "Varela notes that organizational closure, the highest order of feedback, differs from simple feedback in that 'the latter requires and implies an external source of reference, which is completely absent in organizational closure.' Organizational closure involves a network of interconnected feedback loops that is closed and has no inputs or outputs from an outside environment. Instead it feeds upon itself like the recursive snake eating its own tail."[5]

"Please note," says Von Foerster, "this definition of life does not include reproduction. It rejects the belief that reproduction is needed to define living systems. At this moment we are all alive, but none of us are reproducing. We are realizing our autopoiesis. Maturana, Varela, and Uribe would say reproduction is an epiphenomenon of life. To evolve as a race, we must reproduce, but this is a different matter. So reproduction is not the necessary condition for identifying life. Thinking through the implications of autopoiesis may change your attitude toward many problems, like the right-to-life issue."

Von Foerster continues: "Autopoietic systems are autonomous. They determine their own operations. If they fail to do so, they disintegrate and die. Autonomy means 'self-ruling, making one's own laws.' As living systems, each of you is autonomous; you're responsible for your own behavior, for what you say and do. Responsibility, autonomy, and autopoiesis go together.

"Of course, one may argue, 'For heaven's sake, what do you do when you are forced to act against your will? People who have power can make you do things.' The neurophilosophers of Chile answer, 'No, ladies and gentlemen, power is not the cause for other people's behavior. Submission is the cause of power. Somebody can hold a pistol to your forehead and demand your money, but you don't have to give it to him. I'm not saying that he might not shoot you, but this is a different matter. Even with a gun to your head, you still have the freedom to act autonomously.' If you live in Chile, given the political climate, this position may be crucial. This is my philosophical reference to closure. Living systems are autopoietically closed systems. Therefore, they create themselves. They are autonomous!"

CLOSURE OF THE CENTRAL NERVOUS SYSTEM

When an observer describes the nervous system as having independent sensory and motor subsystems that interact with the
environment, he misses the conceptual organization of the nervous system. As Maturana notes, the nervous system is " . . . a
closed neuronal network of interacting neurons . . . all changes
in relative neuronal activity . . . always lead to other changes
in relative neuronal activity. . . . A closed neuronal network
does not have input or output surfaces as features of its organization, . . . given a closed system, inside and outside only exist for
an observer who beholds it, not for the system. . . . The environment where the observer stands acts only as an intervening element through which the effector and sensory neurons interact,
completing the closure of the nervous system."[6]

The concept of neuronal closure is difficult to grasp. We think
the nervous system is open, receiving input from the environment. If, however, as Von Foerster and Maturana argue, the nervous system is closed, it is an "inputless" system. This means that
all of its output becomes its input. Once the system is in operation, nothing enters or exits.

Von Foerster: "One may argue that to say a system has no input is invalid. The question here is: 'What language should one
adopt?' The first man to consider neurologically closed systems
was Ross Ashby. His initial experiments, duplicated by his students and now carried out in Paris by researchers using large
computers, were aimed at examining imputless systems.

"So, the question arises: What is an inputless system? If you
have a system and identify something as an output and make that
output the input, you have an inputless system. This is the beginning of recursive function theory.

"Ashby constructed a system with logical elements that compute logical functions. Each element had two inputs X and Y,
and one output, Z. Z also fed back to the F, changing its mode
of operation. So each element was a nontrivial machine.

"By flipping a coin or other such method, he interconnected
his elements, let's say 20, making each output the input of another
element until all the elements' inputs and outputs were intercon-

nected. Thus he formed a net of computing elements which was completely determined. Obviously, he had to set the initial conditions by setting the output of each element to either a 0 or a 1. Once set, the net was *completely closed*.

"Then he turned on the switch. The machine began to produce a random series of 0's and 1's, but after it ran for eight or ten days, stabilities began to arise, for example, the number 011.

"This was a fabulous result. Nobody could believe his eyes. For instance, Ashby's students observed that the periodicity of this inputless system always produced prime numbers — a periodicity of 3 or 5 or 7. So this was the beginning of systemically closed systems operating recursively."

If we think of the nervous system as closed, as Maturana and von Foerster do, then we are left with a very different view about what we take in or do not take in from the environment. Observing the behavior of self or another, behavior appears purposeful, relative to the environment. We think that we or others gather data (input) with an independent sensory system, process it with the brain, and take appropriate action (output).

Consider a dog trying to escape from its back yard. Finding no exit in the fence, the dog frees himself by digging a tunnel under the fence and escaping. An observer may think the dog acts purposefully. This interpretation implies that the dog has an open nervous system and gathers information from its environment. However, if we view the same behavior assuming the dog to have a closed nervous system, we come up with an entirely different view. The fence is now described as a perturbation (rather than an input), which changes the operations within the dog's nervous system. Restated in computer jargon, the fence is a parametric perturbation. Maturana[7] offers the following example of a pilot using instruments to fly the plane:

> Let us consider what happens in instrumental flight. The pilot is isolated from the outside world (he has no visibility); all he can do is manipulate the instruments of the plane. When the pilot lands, his wife and friends embrace him with joy and tell him: "What a wonderful landing you made; we were afraid because

of the heavy fog." But the pilot answers in surprise: "flight, landing? What do you mean? I did not fly or land. I only manipulated certain internal relations of the plane in order to obtain a particular sequence of reading in a set of instruments."

Finally, let us return to the example of a closed algebraic system. Its elements are the natural numbers and it uses only one operation, addition. In the Maturana sense, we are describing the system's organization. If it is to "live" as a closed system, any change in its structure must be such that its organization is maintained. The question now arises: What happens if we add the operation of multiplication? This is a structural change that maintains the system's organization, its closure. But different things happen to the absolute values of numbers such as 2 and 3 when we change the operation from addition to multiplication. We get 6 instead of 5. The question now arises: Is this change due to an input or a perturbation? Maturana and von Foerster would say this is a perturbation. The change occurs because we have changed the operation within the system.

THE NERVOUS SYSTEM'S DOUBLE CLOSURE

There are two closures in the central nervous system — a sensorimotor closure and a synaptic-endocrine closure. As the reader may remember, the endocrine system participates in the production of neurotransmitters.

Von Foerster comments: "You can imagine what might happen if something interfered with the production of neural transmitters. These substances facilitate the transmission of nerve pulses from the axon to the dendrites. Even the smallest change in the neurotransmitters can markedly affect how neurons function.

"The neural transmitter substances found at the synapses are produced by the endocrine system. The adrenal glands produce steroids and shoot them into the bloodstream for distribution throughout the system.

"We can draw some analogies between communication theory

and the nervous system. First, we have 'station-to-station' communication, the transmission of electrical impulses between neurons. Second, we have 'to whom it may concern' communication by the endocrine system, whose chemical messages affect large groups of neurons simultaneously. These chemical messages are broadcast, to be discriminately used by particular neurons. So the endocrinal system controls synaptic transmission. Now, what controls the endocrine system? It's controlled by the pituitary, the master gland.

"I don't want to burden you with neuroendocrinology. You can find that in any good text. My goal is to underline the interdependence between the central nervous system and the endocrine system. To appreciate the significance of this relationship, I have drawn the following diagram which puts these two systems together in their functional context. Please look at Figure 17.

"The black squares labeled N represent bundles of neurons synaptically connected with each other. Between the spaces of each black box is a thin black line with little lines crossing it; this represents the synaptic gap. On the left side of the figure is a line with arrows marked SS. It represents the sensory surface of the organism, the sum of all the body's sensors. On the right side of the figure is another line with the letters MS, which represents

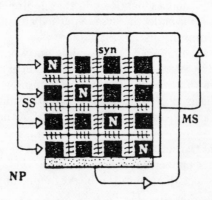

FIGURE 17. Closure of the Central Nervous System in Two Dimensions

the organism's motor system. At the bottom of the figure is a thin, rectangular box with little dots. This represents the pituitary system, the master gland that regulates the endocrine system.

"Nerve impulses traveling horizontally (left to right) ultimately reach and act on the body's motor surface (MS) whose changes (movements) are immediately sensed by the sensory surface (SS). The arrows at the drawing indicate this movement. Nerve impulses traveling vertically (from top to bottom) stimulate the neuropituitary (NP), which releases steroids into the bloodstream. The steroids eventually reach the synaptic gaps, thus modifying the modus operandi of all synaptic junctures. This, in turn, modifies the modus operandi of the entire system.

"The system has two closures: the sensory surface-motor surface closure and synaptic-endocrine closure."[8]

How does this system work?

Von Foerster continues: "I write on the blackboard by moving this piece of chalk which I'm holding in my right hand. This causes excitation of sensors in the retina of my eyes. If I turn my head away from the board, these excitations will change. As a holistic system, I operate on the sensations. Changes in sensation are directly associated with stimuli from the sensory system on the body's surface. So when I want to write on the blackboard, I must bring these two sources of sensory input, my eye and my hand, to a contingency. That means bring them together (correlate them) so I can start writing. I'm acting, so to say, on the stimulation of the surface of my body.

"If you have followed along with me so far, then my next point will not take you by surprise: namely, there must be a gap, an apparent gap, between my sensory surface and my motor surface. For the moment, let me call this gap the 'sensorimotor synapse.' And you can make it as close as you wish. You can close the 'sensorimotor synapse' to a small synaptic gap, which I have done in this doughnut-shaped form in Figure 18.

"I have wrapped the diagram seen in Figure 17 around its two axes of circular symmetry until the artificial boundaries disappear. A torus (doughnut) emerges, having the topology of a dou-

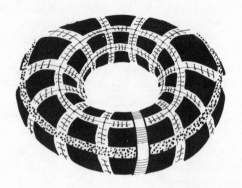

FIGURE 18. Closure of the Central Nervous System in Three Dimensions

ble closure. Here the synaptic gap is the striated meridian in the front center, the neuropituitary the stippled equator: neural and endocrine closure in perfect interaction. This is the organization of a biological entity in a nutshell — or, if you wish, in a doughnut-shell.''

McCulloch and the heterarchy of values

Von Foerster continues: "There is an interesting point associated with this doughnut configuration. It stems from a paper written by Warren McCulloch called 'A Heterarchy of Values Determined by the Topology of Nervous Nets.'[9] McCulloch wondered what behavior might be associated with the circular neural pathways he observed in the brain called 'dromes.' In his paper, he described how the dromes, operating in parallel, would account for value behavior, i.e., how we manifest choice.

"When we are to make a series of choices, is each choice context determined, i.e., relative to the specific instance and context or, as commonly believed, do we choose according to a hierarchy of values? In a hierarchy there is a summum bonum, an ultimate value under which all other values are subsumed.

"'Heterarchy' comes from the Greek word *heteros*. It means

'the other' and *archein* means 'to rule.' So a heterarchy means the rule of one's neighbor. In a heterarchy you rule within a circle. 'Hierarchy' comes from the Greek word *hieros*, which means 'the holy one.' In a hierarchy it is the holy ones, the gods, who rule from the top. McCulloch used the term *heterarchy* to distinguish context-determined value choices from the more familiar notion of a *hierarchy*."

Heterarchical values, expressed in behavior, are relative choices, dependent on time and context. Gregory Bateson used the term "value anomaly" to refer to a situation where a subject makes a series of choices which do not fit our assumption that value behavior is hierarchical.

For example, suppose a subject is asked to choose between apples and bananas; he chooses apples. He is then asked to choose between bananas and cherries, and he chooses the bananas. Finally, he is asked to choose between cherries and apples, and he chooses the cherries. So he prefers A over B. He prefers B over C and he prefers C over A. His value judgments are circular. According to traditional theories of values, this should not be the case. We assume that value judgments must be based on a hierarchy. Our common sense says that heterarchical choices do not make sense. Such behavior is an anomaly.

McCulloch was able to account for the value anomaly by relating it to what he observed in the anatomical structure of the brain. He writes, "The term 'hierarchy' in this context has two implications; each drome (i.e., a circular propagation of a nerve impulse which enters the nervous system via a dorsal root and exits by a ventral root) determines some gain, goal or end, and no two dromes determine exactly the same end."

Like Humberto Maturana, McCulloch looked at anatomy and related it to behavior, thus relating dromic configurations in the brain to value behavior. He states:

> Because organisms live for these ends, they are appreciated by them neither as means to other ends nor as conduct forced upon them, but rather as having that kind of power or importance which culminated in the notion of the sacred or holy — this is the religious

> implication of a "hierarchy" as applied to values. The
> second implication, arising from the sacerdotal struc-
> ture of the church, is that the many ends are ordered
> by the right of each to inhibit all its inferiors. The
> number of ends, although large, is finite. The order
> is such that there is some end preferred to all others,
> and another such that all are preferred to it, and that
> of any three, if a first is preferred to a second and a
> second to a third, then the first is preferred to the
> third. Logically, therefore, to assert a hierarchy of
> values is to assert that values are magnitudes of some
> one kind. Summarily, if values were magnitudes of
> any one kind, the irreducible nervous net would
> map . . . on a plane.[10]

Oversimplified, McCulloch examined two basic ways to in-
terrelate a series of nervous feedback loops, the dromes. In one
case, there was a simple interconnecting set of neurons which
have an inhibitory effect. Thus, if we had four loops, like the
circles of a target, each outer loop inhibits an inner loop. If the
outermost loop fires, all the other loops are inhibited. The inhibition is linear — from top to bottom. It is a one-way causal mechanism.

Conversely, in a heterarchy, the interconnections between the
loops is circular. This is similar to the double closure von Foerster
offers in his topology of the nervous system. There is closure between the sensory and motor surfaces of the body and between
the nervous system and the endocrine system. On a two-dimen-
sional plane, one closure is running from right to left, the second
closure from top to bottom. Wrapped in a three-dimensional
space, however, a surface becomes a torus.

McCulloch concludes that the computational possibilities of
this net are incredibly complex, meta-astronomical, or, as von
Foerster notes, transcomputational. McCulloch writes: "An organism with a net made up of only six neurons which could account for heterarchical choice behavior is sufficiently endowed
to be unpredictable from any theory founded on a scale of values.
It is a heterarchy of values and is thus interconnectively too rich

to submit to a *summum bonum*."[11] (See Figures 17 and 18).

Summing up, McCulloch's work demonstrates that our nervous system is endowed with configurations of neurons that can account for the value anomaly. These are complex mechanisms which do not easily lend themselves to simple logic. Additionally, the notion of relative values is antithetical to organized religions, social and political movements, or any organized group which asserts its *summum bonum*. We are thus inclined to see context-determined choice as anomalous, as pathological, as irrational, rather than as the *sine qua non* neurophysiological condition under which we manifest value in our daily behavior.

RECURSIVE FUNCTION THEORY

Using a mathematical formalism called recursive function theory, we can show that the autonomy of autopoietic systems extends beyond the cellular level to our cognitive and behavioral capabilities. Mathematical formalisms represent systems on paper, making it easier to manipulate and understand them. Recursive function theory is ideally suited to study closure, autonomy, autopoiesis, and biocomputation. It can help us see how closely these ideas are interconnected.

Von Foerster explains: "The formalism I am going to use contains variables and operators. Please don't be alarmed by these terms. They are quite simple. A variable is a conceptual entity whose value can change. Mathematicians represent variables with letters of the alphabet. We're always talking about X's and Y's and Z's. To make life a little easier for you, I will only talk about the X's. To distinguish one X from another, however, I will use subscripted numbers. If we have two X's, I will name them X_0 and X_1 to show that they are different from one another. We use a similar system to name our children. We give each child the same family name, indicating his or her family or origin. We also give each child a different first name to distinguish him or her from the siblings.

"My X's can represent numbers, descriptions, logical propositions, arrays, or arrangements. Almost anything can be represented by X: the arrangement of our chairs, the average salary of everyone in this room. If I want to use X to represent salaries, I can say X_1 represents my salary, X_2 represents the salary of this man sitting directly in front of me, etc. I'm sure you have the idea of how this works.

"Operators act on the variables. The letters Op stand for operators. Operators do things to variables; what they do depends on the variables and the operator.

"If X is a description, the operator will change the description. If X is a number, the operator will change the number. You are all familiar with four operators: addition, subtraction, multiplication, and division.

"Now let me show you two ways to record these operations. Consider the variable X_0. If I want to show an operator (Op) operating on X_0, I write $Op(X_0)$. The result of this operation is written as X_1. The subscript 1 indicates that X_0 has been modified. We write the modified X_0 as X_1. If I repeat the same operation (Op) on X_1, I get X_2. But as I hope you can see, I may also write this as $Op(Op(X_0))$, which is the equivalent of X_2, so:

$$X_2 = Op(Op(X_0))$$

"Let me describe the same process in a more familiar context — an infant playing with a rattle. He puts it in his mouth, chews on it, and rubs it on his face. Each of these behaviors, which we could notate as X, is an operation on his rattle. I could represent the results of this series of operations as X_0, X_1, etc.

"I would like you to consider the following question: Each time the infant engages in one of these behaviors, is the child operating on the same object? I say no. There is no object yet! Why? Because the child does not have a *behavioral* familiarity with what we call a rattle. X_1 is a different experience from X_0 or X_2. So, in this example, Piaget might say the infant does not experience what we call a rattle as a constant. I would say the child has not yet developed sensorimotor competency. I use this term to emphasize the motor behavior that must arise in order for the child to develop a stability of behavior with the rattle. Then it makes full use of the rattle, controls the rattle, knows what to do with the rattle. It has developed sensorimotor competence regarding this particular toy.

"Now I come to a very difficult point. For the child there is no toy; there is only a stable sensorimotor behavior. The child only has access to what is represented on the retina and sensory tactile sensations arising from the operations on the rattle. But since the child can control the rattle, it can anticipate and make predictions about the rattle. It has acquired certain stable behavior regarding the rattle. Sensorimotor competence may now have a name, and the easiest way to name it is to call it a rattle. The thing, however, is also called a rattle. The two, the rattle and the rattle behavior, are complementary. So we have the following equation.

Behavior Name = Object Name"

For example, suppose the "object" under consideration is sound. We can speak of sound as an object in the same sense that a chair or table is an object. Von Foerster gives an example of how sensorimotor competence arose in his own child, who was given a toy trumpet when he was still a baby. "At first he couldn't do anything with it at all. He just put it in his mouth. On one occasion he was breathing out while the trumpet was in his mouth and it produced a sound. The child was absolutely fascinated by this. He played around with it, putting it in his mouth, and again he made a sound. In a few days he could consistently produce a sound from the trumpet. He had developed a sensorimotor competence."

We are now ready to examine what might explain stability arising from a sequence of operations. Why, for instance, does stability arise at all? If each operation on what we call an object is different, how can a stability arise from an infinite sequence of operations? To answer this question we must return to von Foerster's presentation of recursive function theory.

Von Foerster: "We see that $X_3 = Op(Op(Op(X_0)))$, and $X_4 = Op(Op(Op(Op(X_0))))$. You might think this process is unending. I could apply an infinite sequence of operators and go on forever. I cannot, however, diagram an infinite sequence of operations on our variable X. The entire universe would be too small for such a representation.

"Does performing infinite operations on a variable make sense?

Ten years ago the answer was no. Most critics said, 'My dear philosophers, infinite sequences of operations are senseless. They produce nothing. You only succeed in eliminating the initial value of your variable. You never reach the last operation, so you produce nothing. It is a game without end.'"

$$X_{(\infty)} = Op(Op(Op(Op(Op(Op(\cdot \cdot \cdot \cdot \cdot \cdot$$

Von Foerster continues: "Contemplate the expression above and you will notice that 1) the independent variable X_0, the primary argument, has disappeared; 2) that, $X_{(\infty)}$ expresses an indefinite recursion of the operator Op onto operators Op, any indefinite recursion within that expression can be replaced by $X_{(\infty)}$; consequently:

$$X_{(\infty)} = Op(:Op(:Op(\cdot \cdot \cdot \cdot \cdot \cdot$$
$$: \quad : \overline{\qquad\qquad} X_{(\infty)} \rightarrow$$
$$: \overline{\quad} X_{(\infty)} \rightarrow$$

"Now, we come to a crucial step in this argument: An infinite concatenation of operators on operators can be replaced by the simple X_∞. Hence, we could replace the infinite concatenation of operators within one operator by X_∞, *thus transforming an infinite expression into a finite expression, whereby X_∞ is the result of an operation on X_∞.* Hence: $X_{(\infty)} = Op(X_\infty)$.

So $X_{(\infty)}$ is substituted for this never-ending series of operators. This is the crucial step. An infinite sequence *can be transformed into* a finite sequence.

"We can now ask: Are there values which will solve equation: $X_{(\infty)} = Op(X_\infty)$? And, indeed, we find that, certain values can be plugged into this equation, and thus solve it. This equation produces a self-value, similar to the value produced by the sentence, 'This sentence has _____ letters.' The solution to these problems shows that certain *stable* values emerge from infinite recursive computations.

"That is why these values are called 'self values.' The German name for self value is *eigen value*. A continuous sequence of recursive operations (operations on operations) does produce something: eigen values.

"Eigen values are values which fulfill the condition for X_∞. You can also have eigen functions, eigen arrays, eigen arrangements, etc., depending on the primary variable. If the primary variable is behavior, such as an infant's chewing on a rattle, then the infant's operations on the rattle will eventually reach an equilibrium establishing that operation's eigen value: the child's sensorimotor competence in handling a rattle.

"Eigen values produce themselves. This is what happens in autopoietic systems. Operations on the components produce the components. If one operates on anything in a closed algebraic system, it produces those values that are part of its own set. It is the operation that always produces its own entities.

"If you will remember, the nervous system operates on itself. Each neuron fires after performing complex computations. The result of this computation is the input of another neurons' computation. So you can easily substitute the words 'computation of computation' for 'operation on operation.'

"Eigen values may be easier to understand if you can watch them arise before your very eyes. I brought a programmable calculator which I will use to generate an eigen value. We want to see if there is a solution to an indefinite recursive operation when the operation is computing the square root.

"I will program it to calculate the square root of any number you propose. So once it begins, it continuously calculates square roots. You might predict the calculator will go on forever, or, at least, until the batteries wear down. But you will see something interesting happening. In a minute or less, the calculator will stop producing different values. It will stabilize around one value, an eigen value produced by the infinite sequence of operations.

"Would someone give me a number? Ninety-three. Thank you. I will enter 93. I will ask this young man in the first row to press the calculator's start button and begin calling out the results of the calculations. Please tell me the result. We begin with the number 93. OK. 9.64. That looks possible, because the root of 100 would be 10. Now it will calculate the square root of 9.64. What is the next one? 3.11. Now it will calculate the square root of 3.11. It will now go very fast, so just count out the numbers as it calculates the square root of its previous solution. 1.76. 1.33. 1.15. 1.07. 1.04. 1.02. 1.01. 1.00. 1.00. 1.00. 1.00. 1.00. That means, if we take the square root of 1, we get 1.

"So 1 is the eigen value of the operation of a square root. Let's try a different initial value, 75. OK, let's start with 75. 8.66. 2.94. 1.72. 1.31. 1.14. 1.07. 1.03. 1.02. 1.01. 1.00. 1.00. 1.00., etc. The initial value disappeared. It's gone; it's not there anymore. The only thing remaining from this recursive operation is the equilibrium state; the original argument — the primary argument, 75 — has disappeared! Only the eigen value remains. We could get similar results with different operations."

Recursion and cognition

Von Foerster argues that this type of infinite recursion takes place in the nervous system. We have discussed the interaction of the body's sensorimotor system. When we engage in sensorimotor behavior with something, we operate on the object, generating eigen values, more commonly known as the objects of perception.

For instance, consider an infant interacting with what for us is a "ball." After sufficient interaction, he begins to experience the ball as an invariant. His recursive behavior, operating on the result of his previous operations, reaches a stability, just the way the calculator reached its stability.

What is accessible to the child when this occurs? The constructivist would say the child has access to his behavior — his operations and his sensorimotor correlations. The observer, however, sees the child interacting with a thing, a ball.

Unlike the child, the observer dwells in language, a "thing" language. The observer's language nominalizes his own sensorimotor experience, the correlation between the image on his retina and the movement of his eyes. The child only senses the constraints of his actions imposed by what our object language denotes as a ball. These constraints control his behavior and this control must have a particular form.

Push against a chair, and it will "object" to your movement. Interacting with it organizes your sensorimotor behavior. Thus, it is experienced, with the help of language, as object. The chair constrains your behavior, allowing a convergence of sensorimotor behavior to stabilize with respect to that chair (object). This is how the constructivist explains objects.

Objects are *tokens* for eigen behaviors. Tokens stand for something else. In exchange for money (a token itself for gold held by one's government, but unfortunately no longer redeemable), tokens are used to gain admittance to the subway or to play pinball machines. In the cognitive realm, objects are the token names we give to our eigen behavior. When you speak about a ball, you are talking about the experience arising from your recursive sensorimotor behavior when interacting with that something you call a ball. The "ball" as object becomes a token in our experience and language for that behavior which you know how to do when you handle a ball. This is the constructivist's insight into what takes place when we talk about our experience with objects.

Undoubtedly, these objects are experienced as invariant, i.e., as having object constancy. As recursive function theory demonstrates, recursive operations generate "stable" values. Out of an infinity of possible values emerge eigen values. Von Foerster says: "If I were speaking German it would be clearer. The German word for 'object' is *Gegenstand*, denoting something which stands against you — precisely that thing which objects to or limits your behavior. We call that something an object. And this constraint stabilizes our behavior (stable eigen behavior) which we perceive as things.

"There is an additional point I want to make, an important point. Out of an infinite continuum of possibilities, recursive operations carve out a precise set of discrete solutions. Eigen behavior generates discrete, identifiable entities.

"Producing discreteness out of infinite variety has incredibly important consequences. It permits us to begin naming things. Language is the possibility of carving out of an infinite number of possible experiences those experiences which allow stable interactions of yourself with yourself."

Solipsism

Von Foerster continues: "Now that we have achieved these fabulous, beautifully impressive insights into human experience, some of you are probably thinking, 'Heinz Von Foerster is giving us old wine in a new bottle. This is just the old philosophical game of solipsism.' (Solipsists argue that only I exist; everything else is a result of my imagination, a hallucination.) 'Heinz Von Foerster, what do you mean by responsibility? To whom will you be responsible? To yourself? So what? You can always respond to yourself. There is nobody else in your philosophy but you. Ethics and responsibility are meaningless concepts in your solipsistic world.'"

Solipsism, the most extreme form of subjectivism, argues that a person can only know about his own consciousness; when his consciousness ceases, nothing exists. The philosopher C. E. M. Joad explains, " . . . since all our knowledge is of our own mental states, nothing which is other than our own mental states can be known to exist. Now there is no ground for asserting the existence of something that cannot be known. Therefore, my mental states, for all I know to the contrary, constitute the universe. Whether anything in addition to them exists I cannot tell, since being completely within the circle of my own ideas, externally incarcerated in the prison house of my own experience, I cannot penetrate beyond these walls."[12] Although there is no reason to think solipsism is true, Joad notes that it is exceedingly difficult to refute. In fact, it is impossible to refute.

Von Foerster, however, offers the following solution to the charge that constructivism is solipsistic: "Assume I am a successful businessman wearing the bowler hat (Figure 19). As a solipsist, I insist that I am the sole reality; everything else exists only in my imagination. I cannot deny that my imagination contains other people — scientists, businessmen, doctors, housewives, etc. Since they are similar to me, I must grant these apparitions the privilege of being solipsists, of thinking that they are the sole reali-

FIGURE 19. Solipsism

ty and everything and everyone else is a figment of *their* imagination. However, they cannot deny that their imaginations will also
be populated by people — and one of them may be I." So a solipsist may imagine other people who imagine that they are solipsists, i.e., who insist they are the sole reality.

Von Foerster's solution to the solipsist's dilemma is to apply
the principle of relativity. First, he states the principle of relativity in its general form: "A hypothesis that holds for A and holds
for B will be rejected if it does not hold for A and B together."
However, the principle of relativity is not a hypothesis; it can-

not be proved to be either true or false. It is a postulate that one assumes to be true. Thus, to evoke the principle of relativity is a matter of choice.

The principle of relativity can be illustrated with an example from cosmology. For many years, the planet Earth was thought to be the center of the universe. Let us assume that human-like creatures inhabit the planet Mars. Like their counterparts on Earth, they have Mars-centric cosmology. Mars is hypothesized to be the center of the universe. Martian scientists have data that show how everything is rotating around Mars; all the planets are performing in epicycles; they can predict the position of planets, etc.

Scientists from each planet have independently hypothesized a cosmology in which their planet is the center of the universe. Who is right? The planet Earth and the planet Mars cannot simultaneously be the center of the universe. The principle of relativity dictates that the hypothesis "planet centricity" must be discarded. However, if scientists from each planet assert that each of their planets revolves around the sun, i.e., heliocentricity, the contradiction disappears and the principle of relativity admits this hypothesis.

The solipsistic argument contains a similar contradiction. If I am a solipsist, I assume that only I exist. Therefore, I have a problem. Like the man wearing the bowler hat, I have an image of you in my head, and I can imagine you imagining me in your head. In many respects we have identical properties. Both of us, however, cannot be the *only* creatures in the universe. So, if I maintain my solipsistic position, I argue that I hallucinate you, but you are not hallucinating me. You are just an apparition.

The moment I assume that you are also hallucinating me, then principle of relativity says, "No, you can't play that game." You and I can't both be solipsists hallucinating each other.

Von Foerster resolves this contradiction by *choosing* to evoke the principle of relativity. He rejects the solipsistic hypothesis, replacing it with a hypothesis of his own, one which accounts for each of us separately and both together. Von Foerster says: "Now comes the important step of externalization. For instance, in the cosmological example, the heliocentric position postulates the sun as the center of the solar system and the planets, Earth and Mars, as both revolving around the sun. Suddenly, external to the individual planets, a reference frame is being generated, namely, the sun. Returning to the solipsistic dilemma, if I acknowledge the similarity, the identity between myself and the other, and I choose to evoke the relativity principle, I postulate the existence of the outside world!

"The key distinction here is that the usual interpretation of experience is completely reversed. Rather than my experience being a consequence of something outside, i.e., the world, the world is postulated as a consequence of my experience."

Von Foerster writes, "However, it should be noted that since the principle of relativity is not a logical necessity, nor is it a proposition that can be proven to be either true or false, the crucial point to be recognized here is that I am free to choose to either adopt or reject the relativity principle. If I reject it, I am the center of the universe; my reality is my dreams and my nightmares; my language is monologue, and logic mono-logic. If I adopt it, neither I nor the other can be the center of the universe. As in the heliocentric system, there must be a third, a central reference. It is the relation between thou and I, and this relation is *identity*: Reality = Community. What are the consequences of all this in ethics and aesthetics? The ethical imperative: Act always so as to increase the number of choices. The aesthetical imperative: If you desire to see, learn how to act."[13]

This last point warrants further explanation. Von Foerster argues that ethics arise out of choice — in fact, two choices. First, one *chooses* to see identity between oneself and another. Second, one *chooses* to evoke the principle of relativity, thus abandoning the solipsistic hypothesis. This process can only arise from acknowledging another person. The entire process hinges on seeing an identity between oneself and another. The argument will not hold for a bottle or a dog. It is only the identity with another human being that challenges one to find a solution to solipsism. This identity then becomes the basis for ethical behavior. Do unto others as you would have them do unto you. Thus we have the basis for the game of reality.

THE REALITY GAME

Von Foerster goes on: "Now, what game is reality? First, there must be at least two players who want to play it. They create a large board with lots of objects on it which they agree to call 'The World.' Then they put themselves on this board and invent a set of rules for the objects. These rules they agree to call 'The Laws of Nature.' If, during the game, it turns out that the rules they applied in creating the objects don't jive with the rules they invented to play with the objects, they change these objects or change 'The Laws of Nature.'

Now they can play. The goal of the game is for both to agree on how they themselves shall move on the board, even under disagreement. It is clear that A can win only when B wins and vice versa. For if B loses, A is lost, too. Then reality disappears and the nightmares begin.

THE FINAL CLOSURE

One may now legitimately argue: Constructivists dismiss objectivity and attempt to develop an epistemology that is 'inside out.' It starts with the observer and then chooses to postulate or stipulate the outside world. However, constructivism talks about the experience of "thingness" as sensorimotor competence arising from the handling of things! Is this not a contradiction? Is von Foerster saying there are no things out there, but we need to interact with them to build up sensorimotor competence?

Von Foerster responds: "The 'thing' is generated by language and language is addressing itself to somebody else." (This explanation also holds for self-self communication. As Maturana states, "Everything that can be said is said by an observer to another observer, who may be him or herself.") "We are dealing with a very interesting circular argument which depends on the position one takes when making explanations. Sensorimotor competence and objects are two complementary ways of addressing oneself to a particular form of experience, i.e., the experience of thingness.

"Now we come to a most important point. We have two ways

of accounting for the experience of 'thingness,' and both accounts must use language. One, constructivism, argues that experience implies the world; the other, the position of objective reality, argues that the world implies experience. In other words, what is it about this object that accounts for my perceiving it? Now, the primary question: Which position allows one *to account for the emergence of language*?

"The sensorimotor position (the constructivist position) allows you to account for the emergence of language. If you start from the position that objects are already sitting there, in reality, you will be unable to account for the emergence of language. Language becomes purely denotative. This means it simply names the things which already exist. This takes away the miracle of language arising. The constructivist position allows for the ontogenesis of language. The object position is only ontological. This is the essential difference between the two accounts.

"Ontology *will not* address itself to how things came about. Constructivists argue that this excludes accounting for the appearance of certain things. For example, if I look at my navel from an *ontological* point of view, I am unable to explain that funny thing on my stomach. It's a curlicue. Why should it be there? It's useless; it's a joke. There is no way of accounting for this peculiarity on my body.

"Ontogenetically, it is a necessity for my existing. I accounts *for my coming into being*. The ontology accounts only *for me being there*. Ontologically, language cannot account for itself. We need to ask not *what language is*, but *how it emerged*. To ask what language is will always invite us to presume the existence of an objective world. First there were things and then we learned to name them.

"The alternative argument is that language is connotative. When I utter something, I am not referring to something out there. Rather, I generate in you, I touch, so to speak—like a violin player bowing a string, touches you with his music—a whole resonance of semantic correlates. This is what happens when I say 'table' to you. You don't think about a particular table; you think about it as a construct in a semantic-relational network. And you wait to see what I will do with my further utterances with that notion of table—Not with a table. If I say, 'Shall we set the table,' considering the hour you will know exactly what we are going to do—have lunch."

So language has to do with the correlations of behaviors in the nervous system. In Maturana's terminology, this is a second-order behavior. Therefore, it can always be related to the organism. It does not need "things" to account for its coming into being. Of course, the organism is an entity, but this is the self-referentiality of the entire argument.

So "things" take on the nonconstructivist notion of what a thing is, i.e., objects, in language when an observer talks to another observer, who may be him or herself. But the epistemology of confirmation, the epistemology of objective reality, has a problem. I cannot account for the genesis of language. For the objectivist language is denotative; thus, by definition, language must have already existed in order to name it. The denotative view of language can only be ontological.

THE FINAL SUMMARY

So we have come full circle. Chapter 1 began by identifying how we live in language, an object language that generates an objective reality. The notion of objectivity was then examined from epistemological, linguistic, and neurological perspectives. The principle of undifferentiated encoding was also discussed.

Chapters 4 through 7 then addressed the question: Can we account for cognition without first positing the existence of an objective reality? A closed computational view of the nervous system was offered as an alternative explanation for cognition and our experience of reality. Thus, we have two different accountings for cognition.

The problem of solipsism was introduced, the identity of another stipulated, and, by evoking the principle of relativity, the world postulated. The observer's choice to infer the world based upon the experience of perceiving another observer was then offered as the basis for ethical behavior.

The question was then raised: Since these two accountings, these two epistemologies, use and need language, can they account for language? We found that only constructivism's connotative notion of language allows for the emergence of language—second-order behavior arising in a social context.

A denotative language generates an objective reality but cannot generate itself; it cannot account for itself. A connotative language can account for both human experience and the emergence of language.

Thus, this final chapter closes the thoughts in this book by folding Chapter 7 back to Chapter 1, closing this system of ideas—the final closure. Therefore, I would like to suggest that if the reader has the time and interest, it would be extremely useful to reread this book. If one accepts the notion that we are nontrivial machines, then it is but a short step to assume that each recursive journey through these seven chapters will be a different experience.

Appendix

AN INTERVIEW WITH HEINZ VON FOERSTER

Carol Wilder: Heinz, it's a long way from Vienna to the Coast of the Pacific Ocean. I wondered if you could shed some light on the way that brought you here, on some incidents that were influential.

Heinz von Foerster: The first such incident was that I saw the light of day in Vienna on November 13, 1911. It was a Friday. It was a lucky day. I was born into a family which was in itself somehow reflecting the small cosmos that was Vienna before the First World War, a world of movement, ideas, theories, tensions, philosophies, political directions. Remember, Theodor Herzl was the Viennese who started Zionism, Freud was the Viennese who started psychoanalysis; in art the new direction of the Secession and Jugendstil, of the painters Klimt and Schiele, of the architects Otto Wagner and Adolf Loos, of the "Wiener Werkstätte," introduced elements into the cultural life of the time that have not stopped working even today. My own great-grandfather, an architect, did a great urban renewal job, replacing the old fortifications in Vienna by the representative Ringstrasse and, distanced from it, defining urban and suburban regions, a second ring, the

"Gürtel" or belt. This cityscape still works. At the university there were people like Ernst Mark, a precursor to Einstein, who started a revolution in the foundations of physics by his doubts about the concepts of absolute space and time, as seen through Newtonian physics, and Boltzmann, who gave the famous second law of thermodynamics a new interpretation which is still reverberating today. At the same time social concerns were seen and acted upon. The women's cause was taken up by, among others, my grandmother, one of the early suffragettes who founded the first journal in Europe, called *Die Frauenzeit* (Women's Time), completely dedicated to women's liberation. "Teachers' celibacy" was a battle cry of the time, and during my grandmother's lifetime she fought to change the law that forced a teacher in Austria to quit Academy when she became pregnant.

In 1914 the First World War broke out. My father was immediately drafted, together with all the other males of his family and his generation. The Austrian Army, under the command of an ancient emperor, had a peculiarly naive concept of how a war should be fought: you are sitting on a horse, you pull out your saber, you attack the enemy. On the other side the enemy was sitting in trenches and shooting with machine guns. Consequently, the first battles were tragically lost. The two, for me, most influential members of my family, my father and my maternal uncle, were captured in the first weeks of the war. For the next four years I grew up without a father. My mother took me along to wherever she went, mainly to the big country houses of relatives, and I was completely familiar with the world of the grownups around me. Their world was the one of theatre, of art, of journalism, philosophy and science. I did not know it at that time, but I absorbed many things. During one's active life one often handles problems in a certain way, without paying too much attention why, and only in more contemplative periods one realizes that somewhere in the past, perhaps when you were five or six, a respected elder had said, "Live right now. Not in the past, not in the future, here and now."

CW: An impressive example of this for me was when you were talking earlier about your Uncle Ludwig.

HvF: Oh, Uncle Ludwig, yes. Here is a story about a constructed reality, about family legend and the world at large. When I was five or six years old I was taken from time to time to visit an uncle who had designed and built for himself a beautiful house. There was always excellent chocolate, at that time a memorable occasion. Once he asked me what I wanted to be when I grew up. I said, "Ein Naturforscher," a researcher of nature. "Aha," said Uncle Ludwig, "then you have to know a lot." "Yes," I said, "I know a lot." He could have wiped me out, but he said instead: "You may know a lot, but you do not know how right you are." Only now, nearly 70 years later, after having observed children and grandchildren, I know how right he was. When I was 29 and studying at the university, I came upon a book that influenced me (and modern philosophy) deeply and profoundly. It was *Tractatus Logico Philosophicus*, by Ludwig Wittgenstein. Only then I realized that Uncle Ludwig and the author were one and the same. The family did not talk about his philosophy.

CW: But then you became a physicist. How did that come about?

HvF: Very logically — I flunked every other subject. You see, I was not applying myself at all, as it is called today. I just did not study, did not study for exams, did not study for languages, did not study for history. I flunked them all. But mathematics and physics I knew before I was even asked; it was all so obvious and perfectly clear. However, in the "Humanist Gymnasium," as my high school was called, the emphasis was on Greek and Latin and not on mathematics and physics. I only got through high school by the barter system. My neighbors in school were excellent students. They passed me the answers in Latin and Greek, and I gave them the solutions in mathematics and physics. After high school I thought: Let's go on with this thing because it's no problem at all.

CW: I see, it was obvious and natural.

HvF: Yes. On the other hand, there were, of course, things about which I thought: If I knew more and more deeply about them,

I would satisfy some of my basic curiosities: What is going on? What is putting the world together; what is holding it together? If I were to go into biology or any such field and not know what the basic elements of the physical world are, then the biological or psychological work I was interested in would have no foundation. I felt mathematics and logic are the fundamental disciplines for what is the structure of descriptions, and physics for what is to be described as the relation of things to be observed; they would give me some basic background on which I could build my future inquiries.

Maybe I would have turned to biology much earlier than I did if World War II had not forced me to postpone the answers to my curiosities. You could not pursue your own interests then. You had to survive. For me this meant to get out of Austria after Hitler invaded it in 1938. Parts of my family were Jewish. Everybody in Vienna knew that. I could not get a job there. I wanted to marry, I needed a job. The best place for me to go to, I decided, was Berlin. Nobody knew us there. During short stays there I had been impressed by the people, who survived bad situations with *Galgenhumor* (gallows humor). There was no situation in a bitter and soon desperate world of which they did not make fun. I found a job in a research lab. I was supposed to bring proof of my nonexistent Aryan genealogy. I succeeded in postponing it until the saturation bombing of Berlin liberated me from this concern. It also liberated me of all my earthly possessions, some of which I had rather liked and which had been in the family for a long time.

CW: You spent the war years in Berlin?

HvF: Yes, partly, and partly in a medieval monastery in Silesia. It had been secularized in 1820. Since then it had served different purposes, among others as a kind of West Point for the Prussian Army. Now, in 1943, it was transformed into a research laboratory and we had to work there, because our lab in Berlin was bombed. Göring, Hitler's field marshal, had pronounced it illegal to bomb Berlin. Unfortunately, the Allies were not impressed and bombed Berlin nearly into extinction.

CW: But you continued to do research during all this?

HvF: Yes, I was doing plasma physics and I was working on the radar problem, the short wave German radar. It was basic and fundamental research which could not have found application for years to come. That was the whole idea: to stretch out the goal so far that Hitler could not reach for it.

CW: And how did you survive war's end, and what brought you to the USA?

HvF: I was married in Berlin in 1939. We lived there, in the very center of West Berlin and had three children, until our house, together with its neighbor the "Gedächtniskirche" (its ruin is now a war memorial) was bombed into oblivion. Fortunately, we escaped from the bombs and moved to Silesia. We knew it would be a short time before the Russians would chase us from there. The question was only: Would we escape, not only from the Russians but also from the Nazis, who were calling traitors the ones who did not willingly give their lives for the final victory and shooting them on the spot. There were some close shaves, and some unbelievable adventures — too many of them to talk about now.

CW: I still don't know how you found your way to Pescadero.

HvF: I am convinced that I was looking for it with my mind's eye all my life; I recognized it when I saw it, and I clung to it with all my strength.

CW: But there must have been several detours in your 35 years in the US.

HvF: Quite so. I escaped from Berlin, to which I had returned when the Russians took Silesia in April '45. The Russian artillery was bombing the city, which already was burning from saturation bombing. I made my way to Heidelberg, where my wife and children had found refuge with her family. And finally, in 1946

we found ourselves in Vienna. Friends from the US invited me
to come to the US. I arrived in New York in 1949. After years
of starvation diet, mentally and physically, I became immediately drunk with the energy that was driving New York and with
the resulting excitement; it was as if I was on a high all the time.
I had written a little book on memory, I had sent it to friends
in the US; they called me and said I should come to Chicago.
There was a group which was very interested in my work.

I flew to Chicago, Capital Airlines, night flight, $18.00 – all
I could afford. At the University of Illinois Medical School, Department of Neuropsychiatry, there was a towering man, Warren McCulloch, who had started to think of mental processes in
a new way, and he and his people were intrigued by the way in
which I had quantified certain mental processes. My numbers
agreed with the numbers they had measured. I had to give a lecture the same day I arrived. I could hardly speak English, to say
nothing about lecturing. It did not matter. They all listened. If
I groped for a word they helped me. It was intoxicating. In contrast to the culture I came from, it was the content that mattered,
not the form of presentation.

CW: Did this lecture bring about your participation in the Macy
Conferences?

HvF: Yes. My visit in Chicago was in February. Warren invited
me to attend a conference in New York in March.

CW: I heard about these conferences and their participants
through Gregory Bateson. He told me that he took part in one
in 1942, on central inhibition in the nervous system. That was
when the notion of feedback was introduced by Norbert Wiener
and Julian Bigelow. Bateson then went off to war, in the Pacific,
and found that these ideas were staying with him during that
whole period. He said he ran back to the Macy Foundation after
the war and said, "Can we have another one of these conferences?" And Frank Fremont Smith, the director of the conference
program, said: "Warren McCulloch was just here and there is
going to be another one." That began a series of meetings over

ten years of some 25 or so of the best minds from a variety of disciplines. As the conferences progressed you came in and played a central role. Can you tell me about it? What was going on at the Macy Conferences? How do you look at them now?

HvF: I told you about Warren McCulloch, who was head of the Department of Neuropsychiatry at the University of Illinois Medical School.

CW: By training, was he a neuropsychiatrist, a physicist, a philosopher or what?

HvF: The expression "by training" and Warren McCulloch are hard to combine. He was a creative receptacle for every fascinating idea, whether it was logic, mathematics, physiology, neurophysiology, philosophy, or poetry. The best account of himself he gives in his writing is the question: "What is a number that a man may know it, and what is a man that he may know a number?" That question sums up his work physiologically, neurologically, psychiatrically, mathematically, logically, theologically.

I could go on. But let me, for a moment, go back to our meeting in the basement of the Medical School in Chicago. The neighborhood there was a disaster area of poverty, neglect and dilapidation. A few months later, when my family had joined me, the McCullochs drove us around. Our boys, five, six, and eight years of age, looked out of the windows and said, "Chicago has been very heavily bombed!" They had lots of experience and knew a destroyed city when they saw one. But in that basement we were unaware of the surroundings. We were talking about my theory of memory. It was clear that, to make it work, you had to introduce the concept of learning. By recalling what you remember you are feeding it back. With feedback you have a circular causal system, a cybernetic system. So, Warren said, "Heinz von Foerster with his cybernetic idea of memory should come to the Macy Meeting where circular causal feedback mechanisms in biological and social systems will be discussed."

CW: This was in 1949; it must have been the sixth meeting.

HvF: Exactly. Let me give you a brief account of the Josiah Macy Jr. Foundation and the meetings they sponsored. A member of the Macy family had been paralyzed and had been helped by a group of scientists who met at an interdisciplinary meeting. The family consequently decided that they would fund a series of interdisciplinary scientific meetings. The director of the conference program was Frank Fremont Smith, who knew and was highly respected by the scientific community. The problems addressed were of great variety: glaucoma (about which one knew very little at the time), liver illness, aging, etc. There were 10–12 different meetings going on. "Circular Causal and Feedback Mechanisms in Biological and Social Systems" was one of them. The members of this group had met in intervals of half a year five times, so they knew each other very well.

CW: This was their sixth meeting, yet in the volumes published this is Volume No. 1? And you became the editor?

HvF: Yes. At that meeting it was decided to publish the proceedings. After I had presented my theory of memory in English, which by then I had spoken for about four or five weeks, the members of the group had a business meeting. I could not participate; I was a guest. Afterwards they called me and told me that they had decided to publish the proceedings from now on. And, they told me, they all had been appalled by my poor English and had been thinking about a device for me to learn English fast. "We have found a solution," they said. "We decided to make you the editor of these conferences."

It could not have happened in Europe. Only in America.

They were right. I learned English fast. After a month I got about five pounds of green sheets, on which all the conversations were transcribed from the steno tape. I bought the necessary dictionaries and I attacked my task. It was incredible. People like Norbert Wiener or Margaret Mead were speaking already in print. You had not to change a word. Others — including myself — did not make my life so easy.

CW: Who were the participants? Where did they come from?

HvF: Here is the list of people, remarkable, all of them, 30 all together. We will not list all of their names now; just let us look at their disciplines and it becomes clear what excitement their diversity, their different approaches, created. They come from: psychiatry, engineering, physiology, anthropology, computer science, neurophysiology, zoology, psychology, sociology, philosophy, mathematics, biophysics, electronics, and anatomy.

CW: I read through these transcripts and, as I told you at the time, they were the most remarkable intellectual documents I had ever read. The excitement and energy and involvement of these people come clearly through on these pages. I think that the Macy proceedings make a clear case for the move from the metaphors of physical science, of energy, to those of information. Bateson continually argued that the language of physical science is inappropriate to human science.

Could you explain what you think of the limits of technological metaphors applied to human systems? I know that some people take great exception to a behavioral scientist talking about feedback, input, output, analog and digital computation when you talk about human communication, and some hard-line computer scientists think it's a bastardization of their lingo. But here in the proceedings, you talk the language of cybernetics and its application to biological, social and technological systems.

HvF: I have a feeling that the meetings showed a state of affairs like plants pushing up through very hard ground. There were shoots, but not yet flowers. What you watch here, and that is the fascination, is a science in *status nascendi*, in the state of becoming. Usually at big meetings papers are presented, treating popular topics, urgent ones perhaps. Everybody has seen an abstract; they all talk about what they believe they know. But here they were all trying to find out, to get to the ground. Somebody says: "I wanted to report about the spirit of humor." "What do you mean by spirit?" "How do you define humor?" "What do you mean by report?" etc.

CW: In the good Platonic tradition of the symposium. I read them like a mystery story.

HvF: Yes, and nobody finds the solution.

CW: But there are clues . . .

HvF: Exactly, and the clues are found and tossed around. One of the clues is, for instance, the clumsy title of the conference at the beginning. It was obvious that they were looking for something under the umbrella of this complex title which allowed them to question and inform each other about the interests they had at heart.

CW: When did the title change into "cybernetics"?

HvF: When I came to the United States in 1949 Norbert Wiener's book *Cybernetics* had just been published. Warren said to me: "Why don't you read it before you come to the Macy meeting?" So I did. When they appointed me editor of the conferences, I was afraid of the long and clumsy title. I said, "May I make my first motion?" "What is your first motion?" I said, "I would like to call these conferences not 'Circular Causal and Feedback Mechanisms in Biological and Social Systems,' but 'Cybernetics.'" Great applause—they thought it was a good idea. I remember that Norbert Wiener was so touched by the unanimous embrace of his brainchild that he left the room to hide his wet eyes.

CW: Well, it's a synthesizing metaphor for what is going on in the conference, and it does redirect its way.

HvF: Absolutely. Norbert Wiener created this title for his interest in teleological mechanisms. Teleology had become a dirty word among scientists; it belonged to the dark ages. Today a scientist would not talk about teleological mechanisms, a final cause. Efficient cause, yes; final cause, no. But at the Macy meetings the scientists were looking at causal mechanisms, causes in the future instead of the past. They knew it was extremely important to comprehend certain mechanisms, where efficient cause would not bring enlightenment. But they did not know how to incorporate it, what was the language. At one of the conferences John von Neumann became really angry about the misuse and abuse of certain terms that came out of the computer language. One day he had a tantrum. He pounded his fist on the table and shouted, in his expressive Hungarian English: "People, what are you doing?" And he gave, in his anger, an absolutely fabulous account of the distinctions and appropriate applications of the notions of digital, analog, discrete, and continuous. It was superb. The rule of the editing was that everybody got his contribution to the meeting after my editing; at that time they could change whatever they wanted; von Neumann, a perfectionist, thought he really had to elaborate on his presentation, which he had done in anger. I thought he had made all his points very clear, but he chiseled and perfected and elaborated on that presentation. The Macy people, who had to edit the final version, could not get his presentation from him. He delayed again and again; finally they had to go into print without von Neumann's beautiful story. He had pointed out that people had uncritically adopted terms from another field for their special purpose, and often the terms did not fit at all. Think of a carpenter who sees someone using pliers for driving in nails. Can you imagine his language?

CW: Apropos "digital" and "analog." These terms came from both neuroscience and computer science and were used freely at the Macy conferences. Now, they are being used very loosely, by people who study human communication; sometimes digital means language and analog means nonverbal, metaphorical. These are usages which seem intuitively attractive, but I wonder: How can we borrow an expression with a very specific meaning in one field and use it for our purpose in the study of human communication, which is soft and complex?

HvF: In the creative stage of ideas you are allowed to use anything and everything to get things going. Friedrich Schiller, the German poet, liked the smell of rotten apples and, with rotting apples in his drawer, he wrote one beautiful poem and drama after the other. The results: immortal poetry! But the rotten apples are forgotten. In the Macy Conferences you see the rotten apples as well. What comes later is a different thing. As von

Neumann pointed out at the beginning, there are four concepts: digital, analog, discrete, and continuous. These terms were later totally confused, misused here and there, one thing taken for the other. In this experimental stage one is searching for the right conceptual tool.

CW: Yes, I find that some of these terms become a power by themselves, moving along like juggernauts, used in blind devotion: "feedback," "homeostasis," "digital-analog," etc.

HvF: This has the consequence that instead of using language as a tool with which to express thoughts and experience, we accept language as a tool that determines our thoughts and experiences. Maybe when I feel that language is controlling me, then I am beginning to control language.

CW: That brings me to a question I have wanted to ask you for a long time. Feedback is one of the most important concepts at the Macy Conferences, and, as Bateson said, at the first one when the term was introduced, everyone went a bit crazy with the notion of a very powerful idea. You have been very closely identified with the notion of recursion, self-reference, eigen-values, and so on, which to me seems to be feedback coming of age. Could you tell me more about the relationship between feedback and recursion?

HvF: You may remember that in the Macy meetings some problems occurred again and again. They seemed to be attackable by the notion of self-reference, a circular causal circuit. The trouble is, self-reference gives rise to paradox. Therefore, from a scientific point of view, it has to be excluded.

CW: The statement "I am lying," for instance. Not allowed!

HvF: Exactly. Based on the premise that every proposition uttered must either be true or false, the benchmarks of scientific inquiry, you arrive at a system where propositions which are true when they are false and false when true have to be chased out.

They are "verboten." Now, in any type of theory of interaction, say, a theory of communication, or a theory of the brain, of sociology, of language, etc., the observer, the theoretician, must be included in the system he is theorizing about. Take, for instance, one who wants to write a theory of the brain. I think nobody will deny that one needs a brain to write such a theory. Now, in order that this theory can make any claim of completeness, it must be able to account for its being written. That is, a theory that describes the functioning of the brain must, so to say, describe itself or, if you wish, write itself.

At first this sounds crazy. This is because we are usually preoccupied with describing brains of others and not our own. The former task is easy, because any theory will do as long as it is either right or wrong. The type of theory I am talking about has to conform to the extraordinary constraint to describe itself — to turn, so to say, upon itself, the snake biting its own tail. There you have a similarity with feedback. However, recursive function theory goes much deeper. It is precisely the formal apparatus to handle this "turning upon oneself": The meaning of "recursion" is to run through one's own path again. One of its results is that under certain conditions there exist indeed solutions which, when reentered into the formalism, produce again the same solutions. These are called "eigen-values," "eigen-functions," "eigen-behaviors," etc., depending on which domain this formalism is applied — in the domain of numbers, in functions, in behaviors, etc. The expression "eigen-something" comes from the German word for "self." It was coined by David Hilbert in the late 19th century for solutions of problems with a logical structure very similar to the ones we are talking about.

CW: How does that help me to understand people talking? Language?

HvF: The phenomenon "language" is so rich that "understanding" it may have many different aspects. I can see two major schools of thought who look at it very differently. The one wishes to understand the rules of concatenation, by which correct sentences or, in the proper jargon, "well-formed sentences" are strung together. The other one wishes to understand how suddenly the life of one person is fundamentally changed when this person hears some noise produced by someone else, a noise that may in one case sound like "I love you" or in another case "Your sweetheart died." These two schools address themselves to "language" all right, but to two very different functions. The one, I feel, wants to understand monologue; the other, dialogue. What we were talking before, feedback, recursion, eigen-values, etc., can, I believe, contribute nothing to the problems of monologue. However, the conceptual tools to handle dialogue are exactly the ones we touched upon.

CW: What have "Eigen-values" to do with language or dialogue?

HvF: Maybe you will accuse me of playing a talmudic game with you when I say that there are again two cases. One looks at language from an ontological point of view — that is, how language "is"; the other from an ontogenetic point of view — that is, how language arose, how it "became." My view is that monologically and ontologically language cannot be understood at all. I see the problem of language very much the same as the problem of the navel. Ontologically, the navel makes no sense at all. It is a funny, inexplicable curlicue in the middle of our bellies. Ontogenetically, however, we see that it is a necessity: We wouldn't be here without it.

CW: I like your story with the navel very much. But forgive me, what have our navels to do with your eigen-values?

HvF: When you don't see how things become, you may not see how things are. Eigen-values, eigen-forms reproduce themselves recursively. You see them only in the ready-made form, not the way they arose, not the history of their evolution which is now implicitly embedded in their form. This is how I see language — as an Eigen-behavior that evolved through recursive interactions of all of us. A trace of this I can see in the self-referential nature of language itself.

CW: How so?

HvF: I shall call a language only that system of communication that can speak about that system. We have language because we can speak about it. Our vocabulary contains the word "vocabulary," our language has the word "word" and, of course, "language." I don't think that bees have such a vocabulary.

CW: Are you then alluding to "seeing" as seeing oneself seeing oneself. . . .

HvF: I don't think so. I am alluding to "seeing" as seeing oneself through the eyes of the other. If it were otherwise, it would be blindness.

CW: I don't want to end our conversation here, but it has become very late. Thank you very much for your time.

Notes

Preface

1. Fowles, John. (1970) *The aristos: A self-portrait in ideas*. Boston: Little, Brown, p. 8.

Introduction

1. Paladen was a fictional character in *Have gun will travel*, weekly television western series in the 1960's.
2. Varela, Francisco. In Introduction to *Observing Systems*. Seaside, CA.: Intersystems Publications, p. xi.
3. Personal comment from Mental Research Institute colleague, Vin Moley.

Chapter 1: The myth of objectivity

1. Watzlawick, Paul (Ed.). (1984). *The invented reality. How do we know what we believe we know?* New York: W. W. Norton, p. 9.
2. Allen, Woody. (1980). *Side effects*. New York: Ballantine, p. 13.
3. Source unknown.
4. Maturana, Humberto. Lecture "Biology of social systems", given at the Health Science Centre on June 21, 1983, presented by the Family Therapy Program, Dept. of Psychiatry, University of Calgary, Canada. Sponsored by Alberta Heritage Foundation for Medical Research.
5. Ibid.

6. Ibid.
7. Von Glasersfeld, Ernst. (1984). Lecture, Mental Research Institute conference in Munich, Germany.
8. Mahoney, Michael. (1976). *The scientist as subject: The psychological imperative*. Cambridge, MA: Ballinger Publishing Co., p. 3.
9. Capra, Fritjof. (1982). *The turning point: Science, society and the rising culture*. New York: Bantam Books, p. 71.
10. Ibid. p. 53.
11. Matson, Floyd, W. (1964). *The broken image: Man, science and society*. New York: George Braziller, p. 27.
12. Capra, Fritjof. Op cit., p. 57.
13. Ryle, Gilbert. (1949). *The concept of mind*. New York: Barnes and Noble, p. 11–12.
14. Capra, Fritjof. Op cit., p. 60.
15. Rapoport, Anatol. (1968). Foreward in, *Modern Cybernetics Research for the behavioral scientist*, Buckley, W. (Ed.) Chicago: Aldine. pp. xiv–xv.
16. D'Alembert, *Elements de philosophie;* quoted in Matson, Op cit., p. 28.
17. D'Abro, A. (1951). *The rise of the new physics*, (Vol. 1) New York: Dover Press. p. 45.
18. Matson, Floyd W. (1964). *The broken image: Man, science and society*, New York: George Braziller. p. 42.
19. Watzlawick, Paul. (Ed.) (1984). *The invented reality: How do we know what we believe we know?* New York: W. W. Norton, p. 15.
20. Breuer, Rolf. Self-reflexivity in literature: The example of Samuel Beckett's novel trilogy, in Watzlawick, Paul, (Ed.) (1984). *The invented reality: How do we know what we believe we know?* New York: W. W. Norton. p. 145.
21. Planck, Max. (1932). *Where is science going?* New York: Norton. p. 82.
22. D'Abro, A. (1961). *The rise of the new physics*, (Vol. 1). New York: Dover Press. p. 14.
23. Cooper, Lynn A. and Shepard, Rodger, N. (1984, December). Turning something over in the mind. *Scientific American*. Vol. 251, No. 6, p. 106.
24. Mahoney, Michael. Op. cit., p. 129.
25. D'Abro, A. Op. cit., p. 14.
26. D'Abro, A. Op. cit., p. 14.
27. Von Foerster, Heinz. (1981). On constructing a reality. Republished in *Observing systems*. Seaside, CA: Intersystems Publications. p. 295.
28. Restak, Richard. (1984). *The brain*. New York: Bantam Books. p. 51.

29. Eddington, Sir Arthur. (1936). *Science and the unseen world*; Quoted in Joad, C. D. M. *Guide to Philosophy*, New York: Dover Publication. p. 34.

30. Von Foerster, Heinz. (1981). Notes on an epistemology of living things, Republished in *Observing systems*. Seaside, CA: Intersystems Publications, pp. 258–259.

30. Ibid.

32. Piaget, Jean and Inhelder, Barbel. (1969). *The psychology of the child*. New York: Basic Books, Inc., p. 13.

33. Elkind, David (Ed.). (1958). *Six Psychological Studies* by Jean Piaget. New York: Vintage Books. pp. xi–xii.

34. *Webster's New World Dictionary of the American Language* (2nd Edition). (1980). David B. Guralnik, Editor in Chief. New York: Simon and Schuster.

35. *The American Heritage Dictionary of the English Language*. (1969). Edited by William Morris. New York: The American Heritage Company, Inc., & Houghton-Mifflin, Co.

36. Piattelli-Palmarimi, Massimo. (Ed.) (1980). *Language and learning. The debate between Jean Piaget and Noam Chomsky*. Cambridge: Harvard University Press. p. 23.

37. Von Glasersfeld, Ernst. On radical constructivism, in Watzlawick, Paul, Ed. (1984). *The invented reality: How do we know?* New York: W. W. Norton. p. 18.

38. Von Glasersfeld, Ernst. Ibid. p. 24.

39. Varela, Francisco. (1981). Introduction, *Observing systems*. Seaside, CA: Intersystems Publications, p. xi.

40. Von Foerster, Heinz. (1981). Notes on an epistemology of living things. Republished in *Observing systems*. Seaside, CA: Intersystems Publications, pp. 258–259.

Chapter 2: The difficulties with language

1. Wittgenstein, L. *Philosophical investigations*. (1953). Oxford, England: Basil Blackwell, p. 329. Quoted in Brand Gerd, *The Essential Wittgenstein*. New York: Basic Books, (1979).

2. Wittgenstein, L. *Philosophical remarks*. Oxford, England: Basil Blackwell, (1975), p. 5. Quoted in Brand Gerd, *The Essential Wittgenstein*. New York: Basic Books, 1979.

3. Wittgenstein, L. *Philosophical investigations*. Oxford, England: Basil Blackwell, (1953), p. 330. Quoted in Brand Gerd, *The Essential Wittgenstein*. (1979). New York: Basic Books.

4. Bateson, Gregory. (1979). *Mind and nature: A necessary unity*. New York: E. P. Dutton. pp. 60–61.

5. Von Foerster, Heinz. Perception of the future and future of perception. Republished in *Observing systems*. (1981) Seaside, CA: Intersystems Publications. p. 194.

6. Guillen, Michael. (1983). *Bridges to infinity: The human side to mathematics.* Los Angeles: Jeremy B. Tarcher, Inc. pp. 11–12.
7. Guillen, Michael. Ibid., p. 12.
8. Pospesel, Howard. (1974). *Propositional logic: Introduction to logic.* Englewood Cliffs, NJ: Prentice Hall. p. 4.
9. Pospesel, Howard. Ibid., p. 2.
10. Pospesel, Howard. Ibid., p. 1.
11. Guillen, Michael. Op cit., p. 14.
12. Guillen, op. cit., p. 14–15.
13. Frege, Gottlob. *Fundamental laws of arithmetic.* Quoted in Guillen, Michael, Op. cit., p. 15.
14. Bertrand, Russell, *The autobiography of Bertrand Russell*, Vol. I. (1967). London, p. 147. Quoted in Hughes, P. and Brecht, G. *Vicious circles and infinity. An anthology of paradoxes.* (1979). Middlesex, England: Penguin Books. p. 12.
15. Watzlawick, Paul; Weakland, John; Fisch, Richard. (1974). *Change: Principles of problem formation and problem resolution.* New York: W. W. Norton. p. 6.
16. Keeney, Bradford P. (1983). *Aesthetics of change.* New York: Guilford Press. p. 31.
17. Castaneda, Carlos (1972) *Journey to Ixtlan: The lessons of Don Juan.* New York: Simon and Schuster.
18. Ross, W. D. (Ed.). *The works of Aristotle* (Vol. VIII), Metaphysica (2nd Edition). London: Oxford University Press. pp. 1013–1014.
19. Rapoport, Anatol. Foreword in *Modern cybernetics research for the behavioral scientist*, (1968). Buckley, W. (Ed.). Chicago: Aldine. p. xvi.
20. Bateson, Gregory. (1972). What is an instinct?, in *Steps to an ecology of mind.* New York: Ballantine Books. pp. 38–39.

Chapter 3: Maturana and the Observer

1. Maturana, Humberto. Lecture "Biology of social systems," given at the Health Science Centre on June 21, 1983, presented by the Family Therapy Program, Dept. of Psychiatry, University of Calgary, Canada. Sponsored by Alberta Heritage Foundation for Medical Research.
2. Maturana, Humberto. Biology of language: The epistemology of reality, in *Psychology and biology of language and thought: Essays in honor of Eric Lenneberg.* (1976). George A. Miller and Elizabeth Lenneberg (Eds.). New York: Academic Press. pp. 28–30.
3. Keeney, Bradford, P. (1983). *The aesthetics of change.* New York: Guilford Press. p. 18.

4. Maturana, Humberto. Lecture "Biology of social systems," given at the Health Science Centre on June 21, 1983, presented by the Family Therapy Program, Dept. of Psychiatry, University of Calgary, Canada. Sponsored by Alberta Heritage Foundation for Medical Research.

5. Spencer-Brown, G. (1973). *Laws of form*. New York: Bantam Books. p. 104.

Chapter 4: The nervous system

1. Restak, Richard. (1979). *The brain: The last frontier*. New York: Warner Books. p. 20.

2. Ibid., p. 26.

3. Restak, Richard. (1984). *The brain*. New York: Bantam Books. p. 23.

4. Knudtson, P. Painter of Neurons, in *Science 85*, September, 1985, p. 67.

5. Knudtson, Ibid, p. 68.

6. Knudtson, Ibid, p. 69–70.

7. Knudtson, Ibid, p. 70.

8. Fulton, J. F. Physiology of the nervous system. Republished in Von Foerster, Heinz. (1981). Computation in nerve nets. Republished in *Observing systems*. Seaside, CA: Intersystems Publications. p. 48.

9. Von Foerster, Heinz. (1981). On constructing a reality. In *Observing systems*. Seaside, CA: Intersystems Publications. p. 298.

10. Von Foerster, Heinz. Thoughts and notes on cognition. Republished in *Cognition: A multiple view*. (1970). Paul L. Garvin (Ed.). New York: Spartan. p. 43.

11. Piaget, Jean (1970). *Genetic epistemology*. New York: Columbia University Press. p. 18.

12. Langer, Susan. (1951). *Philosophy in a new key*. New York: New American Library.

13. Notes from Association for Advanced Training in the Behavioral Sciences. A private Los Angeles company specializing in courses to prepare psychologists for the California State License exam. Notes from a course given for psychologists in San Francisco, January 1984.

14. Shepro, David; Belamarich, Frank and Levy, Charles. (1974). *Human anatomy and physiology*. New York: Holt, Rinehart and Winston, Inc. p. 142–143.

15. Restak, Richard, M. D. (1979). *The brain: The last frontier*. New York: Warner Books. p. 20.

Chapter 5: Computation

1. Von Foerster, Heinz. (1981). On constructing a reality, in *Observing systems*. Seaside, CA: Intersystems Publications. pp. 234–235.
2. Laing, R. D. (1972). *Knots*. New York: Bantam Books. p. 55.
3. Drawn from tape-recorded conversation with Heinz Von Foerster.
4. Von Foerster, Heinz. (1981). Thoughts and notes on cognition. *Observing systems*. Seaside, CA: Intersystems Publications, pp. 234–235.
5. Pospesel, Howard. (1974). *Propositional logic: Introduction to logic*, Englewood Cliffs, NJ: Prentice Hall. p. 2.
6. Ibid., pp. 19–22.
7. Stevens, John K. (1985, April). Reverse engineering the brain. *Byte-The small systems journal*, Vol. 10, No. 4, p. 286.
8. Von Foerster, Heinz. (1981). Thoughts and notes on cognition. in *Observing systems*. Seaside, CA: Intersystems Publications, p. 238.
9. Weston, P. (1970, August). To uncover; to deduce; to conclude. *Computer Studies in Humanities and Verbal Behavior*, Vol. 3, No. 2, pp. 77–89.
10. Wylie, C. R., Jr. (1957). *One hundred and one puzzles in thought and logic*. New York: Dover Press.
11. Ashby, Ross. (1968). Principles of the self-organizing system, in *Modern cybernetics research for the behavioral scientist*. Buckley, W. (Ed.). Chicago: Aldine. pp. 110–111.
12. Buckley, W. (Ed.). *Modern cybernetics research for the behavioral scientist*. Chicago: Aldine. p. 70.
13. Von Foerster, Heinz. (1981). Molecular ethology: An immodest proposal for semantic clarification. In *Observing systems*. Seaside, CA: Intersystems Publications. pp. 154–155.

Chapter 6: Biocomputation

1. Stevens, John K. (1985, April). Reverse engineering the brain. *Byte-The small systems journal*, Vol. 10, No. 4, p. 286.
2. McCulloch, W. S. and Pitts, W. (1943). A logical calculus of ideas immanent in nervous activity. *Bulletin of Math Biophysics*, Vol. 5, No. 115.
3. Von Foerster, Heinz. (1981). Computation in nerve nets. Republished in *Observing systems*. Seaside, CA: Intersystems Publications. p. 35.
4. Von Foerster, Heinz. (1981). On constructing a reality. Republished in *Observing systems*. Seaside, CA: Intersystems Publications. pp. 303–304.

5. Lettvin, J. Y.; Maturana, H.; McCulloch, W. and Pitts, W. (1959). What the frog's eye tells the frog's brain, in the proceedings of the Institute of Radio Engineers (Vol. 47). pp. 1940–59.
6. McCulloch, W. S. and Pitts, W. Op cit.
7. Von Neumann, John. The general and logical theory of automata. In *Cerebral mechanism in behavior*. Jeffres, L.A. (Ed.), New York: John Wiley & Sons. p. 1.

Chapter 7: Closure

1. Varela, Francisco J. (1984). The creative circle: Sketches on the natural history of circularity. In *The invented reality: How do we know what we know?* Paul Watzlawick (Ed.). New York: W. W. Norton. p. 318.
2. Watzlawick, Paul; Beavin, Janet and Jackson, Don D. (1967). *Pragmatics of human communication*. New York: W. W. Norton. p. 123. Watzlawick quotes Spengler, Oswald. (1926). *The decline of the west, form and actuality* (Vol. 1). New York: Alfred Knopf, Inc.
3. Andrew, A. M. (1979). Autopoeisis and self-organization. *Journal of Cybernetics*. 9, p. 359.
4. Varela, F. J. (1979). *Principles of biological autonomy*. New York: Elsevier North Holland. p. 13.
5. Keeney, Bradford, P. (1983). *The aesthetics of change*. New York: Guilford Press, p. 84.
6. Maturana, Humberto. Lecture "Biology of social systems," given at the Health Science Centre on June 21, 1983, presented by the Family Therapy Program, Dept. of Psychiatry, University of Calgary, Canada. Sponsored by Alberta Heritage Foundation for Medical Research.
7. Maturana, Humberto. (1976). Biology of language: The epistemology of reality, in *Psychology and biology of language and thought: Essays in honor of Eric Lenneberg*, George A. Miller and Elizabeth Lenneberg (Ed.). New York: Academic Press. p. 42.
8. Von Foerster, Heinz. (1981). On constructing a reality. Republished in *Observing systems*. Seaside, CA: Intersystems Publications. pp. 304–305.
9. McCulloch, W. S. (1969). A heterarchy of values determined by the topology of nervous nets, in McCulloch, W. S.: *Embodiment of mind*. Cambridge, MA: M.I.T. Press. pp. 40–43.
10. Ibid.
11. Ibid.
12. Joad, C. D. M. (1936). *Guide to philosophy*. New York: Dover Publications. p. 56.

13. Von Foerster, Heinz. (1981). On constructing a reality. Republished in *Observing systems*. Seaside, CA: Intersystems Publications. pp. 307–308.

Figures and tables

1. Fig. 1: Freehand sketch by Heinz von Foerster.
2. Fig. 2a: Clarke, E. and Dewhurst, K. (1979). *An illustrated history of brain function*. CA: Univ. of California Press.
3. Fig. 2b: Ibid. (Fig. number in original text is 120).
4. Fig. 3: Ibid.
5. Fig. 4: Clarke, E. and O'Malley, C. D. *The human brain and spinal cord*. CA: University of California Press. p. 331.
6. Fig. 5: Drawn by Lebbeus Woods for Heinz von Foerster. Von Foerster, Heinz (1981). On constructing a reality. Republished in *Observing systems*. Seaside CA: Intersystems Publications. p. 297.
7. Fig. 6: Shall, D. A. (1956). *The organization of the cerebral cortex*. London: John Wiley. (Fig. number in original text is 2.)
8. Fig. 7: Drawn by Heinz von Foerster, in Von Foerster, Heinz. (1981). On constructing a reality. Republished in *Observing systems*, Seaside, CA: Intersystems Publications. p. 299.
9. Fig. 8: Noback, Charles R. (1967). *The human nervous system: Basic elements of structure and function*. New York: McGraw-Hill. p. 49. Original figure number is 3-1.
10. Table 1: Constructed by Heinz von Foerster.
11. Table 2: Ibid.
12. Fig. 9: In Von Foerster, Heinz. (1981). Technology: What will it mean to librarians?, Republished in *Observing systems*. Seaside, CA: Intersystems Publications. p. 219.
13. Fig. 10: Drawn by Heinz von Foerster.
14. Fig. 11: Ibid.
15. Table 4: Constructed by Heinz von Foerster.
16. Fig. 12: Computation in neural nets, in *Currents in modern biology*. (Vol. 1, No. 1). Amsterdam: North-Holland Publishing Company. p. 56.
17. Fig. 13: Ibid., p. 57.
18. Table 5: Ibid., p. 59.
19. Fig. 14: Drawn by Heinz von Foerster.
20. Fig. 15: Ibid.
21. Fig. 16: Ibid.
22. Fig. 17: Drawn by Rodney Clough for Heinz von Foerster, in Von Foerster, Heinz. (1981) On constructing a reality, Republished in *Observing systems*. Seaside, CA: Intersystems Publications, p. 305.

23. Fig. 18: Ibid.
24. Fig. 19: Drawn by Gordon Pask for Heinz von Foerster in Von Foerster, Heinz. (1981). On constructing a reality, Republished in *Observing systems*. Seaside, CA: Intersystems Publications. p. 307.

Index